T0306065

An Introduction to Health Information Technology in LTPAC Settings

An Introduction to Health Information Technology in LTPAC Settings

Gregory L. Alexander, PhD, RN, FAAN
John F. Derr, RPh, FASCP
Lorren Pettit, MS, MBA

CRC Press
Taylor & Francis Group
Boca Raton   London   New York

CRC Press is an imprint of the
Taylor & Francis Group, an **informa** business
A PRODUCTIVITY PRESS BOOK

CRC Press
Taylor & Francis Group
6000 Broken Sound Parkway NW, Suite 300
Boca Raton, FL 33487-2742

First issued in paperback 2021

ISBN-13: 978-1-03-209506-6 (pbk)
ISBN-13: 978-1-138-03914-8 (hbk)

Library of Congress Cataloging-in-Publication Data

Names: Alexander, Gregory Lynn, 1961- author. | Derr, John F., author. | Pettit, Lorren, author.
Title: An introduction to Health Information Technology in LTPAC Settings / Gregory L. Alexander, John F. Derr, and Lorren Pettit.
Description: Boca Raton : Taylor & Francis, 2018. | Includes bibliographical references.
Identifiers: LCCN 2018009309| ISBN 9781138039148 (hardback : alk. paper) | ISBN 9781315176086 (ebook)
Subjects: | MESH: Medical Informatics | Long-Term Care | Subacute Care
Classification: LCC R858 | NLM WX 26.5 | DDC 610.285--dc23
LC record available at https://lccn.loc.gov/2018009309

Visit the Taylor & Francis Website at
http://www.taylorandfrancis.com

and the Productivity Press site at
http://www.ProductivityPress.com

HIMSS Mission

To lead healthcare transformation through the effective use of health information technology.

Printed in the U.S.A. 5 4 3 2 1

Requests for permission to make copies of any part of this work should be sent to:
Permissions Editor
HIMSS
33 W. Monroe St., #1700
Chicago, IL 60603-5616
nvitucci@himss.org

The inclusion of an organization name, product, or service in this publication should not be considered as an endorsement of such organization, product, or service, nor is the failure to include an organization name, product, or service to be construed as disapproval.

For more information about HIMSS, please visit www.himss.org.

To my wife, children, parents, and siblings, who have always been supportive of my work and me. As I get older, I realize more and more the value of having good support systems like you in my life.

Finally, to my research team, faculty, and collaborators, who have helped me remain focused, dedicated, and steadfast in my research career, thank you for sharing valuable insights and sticking by my side.

Greg Alexander

To my wife (Polly) and daughters (Deborah and Jennifer), who supported me throughout my 50 years of work in healthcare. To my departed Father who owned a Community Pharmacy and taught me the value of healthcare since I was eight years old.

Also, to my fellow healthcare professionals that I have had the privilege of working with and their dedication to the quality of care of seniors.

John Derr

To my wife (Diana), boys (Aaron and Brendan), and the newest member of the Pettit family (Lilliana), who was born during the birth of this textbook. I am truly blessed.

Lorren Pettit

Contents

Foreword xiii
About the Authors xxiii
Introduction xxvii

SECTION I   GENERAL ENVIRONMENT

1   **LTPAC and the Healthcare Environment** **3**
    Learning Objectives 3
    Introduction... 3
    Patients/Consumers... 5
    U.S. Payers and Providers..................................... 7
        Payers... 8
        Healthcare Providers 9
        Healthcare Provider Organizations........................10
        Ancillary Medical Services................................15
        Alternative Payment Models (APMs)........................15
    Oversight 16
        Laws and Regulations 17
        Regulatory Bodies 20
    Summary 22
    For Discussion..23
    References 23

2   **LTPAC and the Technology Environment** **27**
    Learning Objectives 27
    Introduction..27

Technology Infrastructure 30
  Data 30
  Routers, Switches, Servers...30
  Wired and Wireless Networks 31
  Client Terminals and (Portable) Devices 32
  Data Storage and Data Integration 33
Applications...34
  Administrative Applications 34
  Financial Applications...35
  Clinical Applications 36
  Application Standards and Interoperability..................41
  Health IT Standardization..43
Technologies for LTPAC Settings 44
Information System Maturity 46
Summary 48
For Discussion...50
References 51

SECTION II SYSTEMS

**3 LTPAC and the Health IT Life Cycle: Decision,
   Selection, and Acquisition 55**
Learning Objectives 55
Introduction...56
Decision...57
  Define the Problem...59
  Determine the Cause 61
  Identify Solutions 61
Selection 63
  Preliminary Investigation 63
  Requirements Analysis...65
  Analysis of Alternatives..72
  Proposal/Approval...72
Acquisition...73
  Build 75
  Buy..75

Summary 78
For Discussion 80
References 80

**4 LTPAC and the Health IT Life Cycle: Project
Management 83**
Learning Objectives 83
Introduction 84
Pre-Implementation 84
   Planning 85
   Change Management 86
   Implementation Strategies 86
   Solution Customization 87
   System Integration 93
   User and Operational Manuals and Training 94
   Activation 94
Implementation 95
Post-Implementation 96
   Managing Normal Healthcare Information Systems
   (HIS) Operations 96
   Managing Disrupted Health Information Systems
   (HIS) Operations 97
Summary 98
For Discussion 99

5 Privacy and Security in LTPAC Settings 101
Learning Objectives 101
Introduction 101
The CIA Triad 102
   Confidentiality 102
   Integrity 103
   Availability 103
Data Governance 104
Data Management Controls 105
Data Management and User Access Controls 106
Risk 107
Disaster Recovery and Business Continuity Plan 108

Summary 109
For Discussion 110
References 110

SECTION III   ADMINISTRATION

6 Management and Leadership 115
Learning Objectives 115
Introduction 116
Leadership 117
  Setting a Strategy 117
  Championing Culture 119
Leadership Archetypes 120
Leadership Guardrails 121
  Business Operations 122
  Legal and Regulatory Compliance 123
  Business Ethics 124
Management 124
  Managing Operations 124
  Managing Staff 131
  Managing External Relationships 138
Summary 140
For Discussion 140
References 141

SECTION IV   OTHER CONSIDERATIONS

7 LTPAC and Future Considerations 145
Learning Objectives 145
Introduction 145
Valued Quality Coordination of Care 148
VQCC #1: Duration of Care 148
VQCC #2: eAssessments 149
VQCC #3: Chronic Care Comorbidity Care 149
VQCC #4: Medication Management 150
VQCC #5: Technology 150
Future Trends 151

Person-Centered Models 151
Person-Centered Outcome Measures 158
Person-Centered Partnership Measures...................... 159
Person-Centered Experience Measures 159
Longitudinal Health Records 160
Value Propositions for Technology in LTPAC................ 161
The Future of LTPAC...................................... 163
Conclusion.. 164
For Discussion.. 164
References 165

8 International Perspectives on LTPAC HIT 169
Learning Objectives 169
Introduction.. 169
International Commonwealth Fund 170
Surveying International Landscapes........................ 171
North America... 172
Australia... 182
Asia 183
Europe 184
Conclusion.. 185
For Discussion.. 185
References 186

Index 191

Foreword

For many, the world of long-term and post-acute care, or "LTPAC" for short, is a "black box" which can be addressed with a "one-size-fits-all" approach. Indeed, many healthcare professionals do not have a basic understanding of what type of organizations are labeled LTPAC, what services are and are not performed, or why LTPAC sites accept some patients for admission and reject others. Nor is there a clear understanding outside LTPAC circles of the reimbursement models and incentive plans driving operational behaviors. Add to these challenges the variances between the types of LTPAC provider organizations involving financial incentives, payment models, quality measures, and regulatory requirements. Add it all up and a "one-size-fits-all" approach admittedly looks very attractive.

The LTPAC world is a complex yet critical component of the US healthcare ecosystem. Moreover, this world is growing in importance, as a wide spectrum of healthcare organizations are waking to the fact that their organizations must effectively interact with LTPAC organizations in order to remain effective and competitive. By extension, health information technology (IT) workers familiar with the intricacies of the LTPAC world will play a significant role in the success of this emerging integrated ecosystem. To fully appreciate the operational motivations of LTPAC organizations and the role health IT plays, it is important for the reader to understand both the anatomy of LTPAC (what it's made of), as well as its "physiology" (how these parts work individually and collectively). First, the "anatomy" of LTPAC and a review of its constituent parts.

There are five components that have traditionally been included in LTPAC:

a. *Long-term acute care hospital (LTACH)*: A hospital level of care for individuals with complex medical conditions that require intensive management, the "chronically acutely ill" with multi-organ failure. These are the sickest of the sick. LTACHs have 24 hour physician coverage, approximately 4–6 hours of nursing care per patient per day, onsite pharmacy lab, radiology, telemetry, and a mini-ICU with intensive nursing coverage. Barriers to admission include the requirement for a 3-day ICU stay, daily physician oversight, and a high likelihood of a 25-day length of stay (LOS).

b. *Inpatient rehabilitation facility (IRF)*: A hospital level of care for individuals principally needing complex, intensive rehabilitation services for conditions such as stroke, spinal cord injury, and traumatic brain injury. IRFs have 24 hour physician coverage, approximately 4 hours of nursing care per day, onsite pharmacy lab, and radiology and telemetry capability. Barriers to admission include finances and the ability to tolerate 3 hours of rehab per day.

c. *Skilled nursing facility (SNF)*: A less-than-hospital level of care for individuals with established medical and surgical issues requiring skilled therapy services to improve function. Physician coverage varies from daily to once every 1–2 weeks, and there is an average of 2 hours of nursing care per day. Lab, X-ray, and pharmacy services are all off site. SNFs have little capability to manage acute or complex issues. The average LOS is 24 days.

d. *Home health agency (HHA) (AKA visiting nurse association)*: A home-based provider of nursing, therapy, and care coordination services to individuals who are home bound. HHAs can manage intravenous therapy, complex wounds, and chronic conditions such as CHF, diabetes, and COPD. They provide on average 15 visits over a 60-day episode of care. Physician oversight is provided by community physicians.

e. *Hospice*: End of life services including palliative care, counselling, and bereavement services for individuals who have been determined to have a high probability of dying within 6 months. These services can be provided in a hospital, a designated hospice facility, an SNF or extended care facility (ECF), or at home. Visits are episodic, and there is heavy reliance on family or facility staff to provide basic care.

With the advent of new payment models there are two other long-term care sectors that are often added to LTPAC:

f. *Home- and community-based services (Medicare) (HCBS)/long-term services and supports (Medicaid) (LTSS)*: Meals on Wheels is perhaps the best-known service. Others include home-maker, home health aide, transportation, and housing modifications. These services are often engaged and coordinated by HHAs. They address specific needs that the individual is unable to meet. These services fill in the gaps between what individuals can do and what their living environments require them to do to be able to stay at home safely. There are income caps that limit eligibility; however, these services can usually be purchased regardless of income.

g. *Assisted living facilities (ALF)/continuing care retirement communities (CCRC)*: These are two common housing options that also provide some support services and some medical care in the same venue. The goal is to provide sufficient services for the elderly to be able to "age in place" and not transfer to a nursing facility as their functional needs increase. The barriers to access are largely financial. Because they represent relatively "low cost" settings, they are increasingly medicalized with the goal of avoiding higher cost sites of care.

The grid in the below table compares the approximate *range* and *intensity* of capabilities among these different entities (L = low range/intensity; M = medium range/intensity; H = high range/intensity).

	Complex Procedures	Physician Intensity	Nursing Intensity	Therapy Services	Supportive Services
Acute Care Hospital	H	H	H	M	L
LTACH	M	H	H	M	L
IRF	M	M	M	H	M
SNF/ECF	L	L	M	M	M
HHA	L	L	L	M	M
Hospice	L	L	L	L	M
HCBS/LTSS	L	L	L	L	H
ALF/CCRC	L	L	L	L	H

Although there is a general gradient in the types and intensities of services offered in these sites, LTPAC was not designed to provide individuals with a logical pathway to recovery. Instead, the anatomy was driven largely by the financial incentives under fee-for-service (FFS) payment models for both acute care hospitals and LTPAC providers. These financial incentives drive the "physiology" of this healthcare sector which is not a system, but rather a federation of unrelated service providers, each working independently from the others but mutually dependent on referrals from the other sites. And the financial incentives are different for each LTPAC player.

The acute care hospitals are paid a fee at discharge based on a table of Diagnosis-Related Groups (DRGs). The payment is based on the conditions treated during the stay and is the same regardless of the length of stay. Whether the patient stays 10 days or 3 days does not change the payment. As a result, hospitals quickly learned to discharge patients as soon as possible to make room for new admissions. LTPAC grew as hospitals discharged patients (hence the term "Post-Acute") with a wide variety of clinical and functional needs as quickly as possible to shorten LOS and maximize the number discharges and associated payments.

Each LTPAC sector has a different FFS incentive. LTACH and IRF are paid on a DRG-type model but with different payment scales. IRFs can shorten their ALOS to point but must demonstrate specific functional gains during the stay. The incentive for IRFs is to admit patients with a high probability of making significant functional gains in the shortest time possible. LTACHs, on the other hand, must manage their ALOS to be 25 days as a condition of participation in Medicare, their principal payer. Accordingly, their incentive is to admit patients who meet admission requirements and who need on average 25 days of intensive services.

SNFs are not paid by discharge. They are paid a daily rate based on Resource Utilization Groups (RUGs). If a SNF can justify the need for skilled therapy services, Medicare will pay for up to 100 days. The incentive for SNFs is exactly the opposite of the incentive for acute care hospitals. SNFs maximize their revenue by keeping the patient in the SNF for as long as possible. Since this daily payment is all inclusive, their other incentive is to avoid patients who require expensive medications or equipment, or require high levels of nursing services.

Home Health Agencies have yet another payment model and set of incentives. They are paid based on a 60-day episode of care with the payment determined by Home Health Resource Groups. There is no limit to the number of episodes if the individual continues to meet eligibility requirements. Each episode requires a minimum number of services. The challenge for the HHA is to meet the needs of its service area without triggering adverse quality outcomes or providing too few or too many services.

Under FFS, each part of the healthcare system operates in its own self-interest to maximize revenues. Some incentives limit the transfer of patients from one site to the next level of intensity. As a result, there are patients in each level of care for whom there are no available alternative sites of care. The most frequent consequence is transfer back to the hospital, which has become a high cost pathway for getting LTPAC services.

Because LTPAC under FFS is a federation and not a system, there is little urgency to communicate well, coordinate care, or integrate services in a way that improves quality, safety, or cost. Maximizing revenues for each site takes precedence over lowering costs for the entire system. The readmission penalty for acute care hospitals has changed this calculus somewhat. Because of this penalty, hospitals have become more selective about where they discharge patients and avoid those sites with high readmission rates which might trigger the penalty. However, hospitals still have a stronger incentive to discharge patients as quickly as possible. The readmission penalty has spurred the development of "preferred provider networks" in areas with an abundance of LTPAC providers. Preferred providers take patients in transfer sooner and keep them from returning before 30 days.

This trend towards greater selectivity has accelerated because of the growing impact of alternative payment models (APMs) which not only turn the FFS physiology upside down but create other criteria for preferred providers. The percent of total healthcare payments by APMs has increased from 15% in 2017 to nearly 30% in 2017.

The most common APMs are:

a. Population-based models including Medicare Advantage Plans and accountable care organizations (ACOs)
b. Bundled payment models which set an all-inclusive fee for care provided for specific period after a triggering event such as joint replacement

c. Disease-specific models for end-stage renal disease (ESRD) and oncology

d. Comprehensive primary care models (medical home) which pay certified practices for the additional costs of care coordination and preventive services

Under APMs, service providers receive payment based on outcomes achieved for a population of enrollees rather than on the number of services delivered. Providers all share a common incentive to provide all the services that are necessary to achieve good outcomes at the lowest possible cost. To increase revenue under an APM, a provider must increase the number of individuals it is responsible for rather than increase the number of services provided. Furthermore, the provider must manage the care of their patients as efficiently as possible at the lowest overall cost while achieving the mandated quality outcomes. Whereas revenues under FFS are a variable and can be increased by increasing the number of services, revenues under APMs are fixed. Because cost is the only variable under the provider's control, APMs require efficient care which achieves high quality at the lowest cost.

APM are driving the new "physiology" for LTPAC, and they are creating new configurations of services driven by a new set of financial incentives. APMs have strong incentives to identify their members who are most likely to require many resources. Healthcare costs are unevenly distributed, such that 1% of the population requires nearly 25% of all resources and 5% requires nearly 50%. One strategy adopted by APMs is to focus on the utilization of the top 5% through improved identification, management, care coordination, and use of alternative sites of care to provide needed services at the lowest possible cost.

For LTPAC this means, among other things, that "post-acute care" is no longer an accurate term. Increasingly, the entities "previously known as LTPAC" are providing services in lieu of acute care or with the goal of avoiding hospitalization.

Because of their relatively high costs, LTACHs and IRFs are likely to see fewer referrals as APMs become more widespread. HAA and SNF, on the other hand, as relatively low-cost alternatives, will likely see an increase in utilization as they add capabilities that allow them to safely replace higher cost sites of care.

As an example of this trend, many HHAs are adding physicians and advanced practice nurses to provide greater clinical intensity at home. They are providing chronic care management, which was not a covered benefit under Medicare but is a cost-effective approach for managing frail, home-bound, potentially high-cost elders under an APM. Hospital at Home, Mobile Observation Units, and the use of telemetry are likely to become more common and help move more care to home and out of hospitals, LTACHs, IRFs, and SNFs.

For SNFs, the growth of APMs is driving changes that are even more dramatic. Medicare Advantage plans have achieved an SNF ALOS that is 40% shorter than under FFS payments while achieving the same outcomes. As the reach of APMs increases, SNFs will come under increasing pressure to shorten LOS to the same levels. It is likely that 40% of SNFs will go out of business as APMS eliminate the non-value-added cost of long SNF stays. The 60% of SNFs that remain will have learned to reduce LOS and add clinical capabilities that the APMs find attractive, such as increased clinical intensity with 7-day per week physician/advanced practice nurse coverage, direct admissions from the emergency department, reduced readmissions, and new clinical capabilities such as telemetry and ventilators.

Each APM has a population of individuals with complex medical, behavioral, and functional issues (the 1%). Previously they would have required hospitalization and then transfer to LTPAC for further care. Now, some of these individuals go directly from home to SNF with or without an intervening emergency department visit and without hospitalization. They will stay at home longer and leave SNFs sooner because of home- and community-based services coordinated by an HHA.

The new APM-based organizations will be rewarded to the extent they can function as coordinated, integrated systems even though they are made up of disparate parts with different owners. The teams that provide care to these complex individuals will be larger because they include HHAs, SNFs, HCBS providers, and behavioral health providers. These larger teams make it easier to address some of the social determinants of health such as poor housing, transportation, and inadequate home supports, which contribute a disproportionate share of the costs of care. The APM driven care systems will be more complex because they must coordinate the activities of all the constituent parts to efficiently meet the extensive care needs of their most complex patients.

In addition to providing a broader range of services often with increasing intensity, HHAs and SNFs will likely be given the important role of guiding these new care systems towards more person-centered care. HHAs and SNFs engage the individual during episodes that last weeks compared to days for the hospital or minutes in the office. Increasingly it will fall to them to help individuals clarify what matters most to them, establish advance directives, and perform comprehensive evaluations of cognition and function. These are critical contributions to care that are largely missing in the current FFS system: interventions which establish the individual's priorities and shape the actions of the healthcare system. HHAs and SNFs will also assume a major role in establishing and transmitting a comprehensive care plan to the next responsible provider.

Increasingly health IT will play an enabling role as these new healthcare arrangements evolve. Often it will serve as one of the drivers for shared governance when there is no common ownership but a requirement for increased coordination. Health IT will make it possible to efficiently share increasing amounts of data needed for safe transitions of care and longitudinal coordination of care across multiple sites and care teams. And it will power the analytics needed to guide these new organizations.

The issues discussed in this book lay the foundation for the next era in healthcare based on health IT enabled care integration and coordination. The growing cadre of acute care providers based outside of hospitals in LTPAC settings will succeed only to the extent that they able to use data from and contribute data to the other sites that participate in an episode of care. The authors provide detailed guidance in all phases of health IT from needs assessment to implementation and maintenance. Their contribution is timely and extremely welcome.

Terrence A. O'Malley, M.D.
Federal HIT Advisory Committee
Co-chair U.S. Core Data for Interoperability Task Force (USCDI)
Massachusetts General Hospital
Partners HealthCare System, Inc.
Boston, MA

About the Authors

Dr. Gregory L. Alexander's (PhD, RN) greatest nursing contributions are in gero-informatics research. His research incorporates cutting-edge IT innovations used to assess, monitor, and improve the health of older adults. Alexander is for the first time conducting research to design a national long-term-care IT maturity model to estimate the impacts of IT adoption trends on quality measures. He has created novel IT systems using markerless human motion capture systems to evaluate functional status in vulnerable populations. He leads pioneering IT evaluations, benchmarking IT effects on quality of nursing home care, an area where scant research exists. He works with multidisciplinary teams patenting designs for wireless sensor systems used to foster independent living for frail elders. These technologies are having profound sustained effects in real-life settings occupied by nurses and their patients. Critical outcomes include new ways of performing nursing assessment and communicating about chronic conditions resulting in improved quality measures. His research informs national and international health policy initiatives. He has presented this work nationally and internationally.

John Derr (RPh, FASCP), is the Chief Consumer Affairs Officer of CareCommunity, a MatrixCare person-centric software platform. He has over fifty years of executive-level experience in most facets of healthcare. He has held top executive-level positions with E. R. Squibb & Sons (Director of Product Development and Strategic Planning); Siemens (Vice President and Division Manager for Ultrasound and Nuclear Medicine); and National Medical Enterprises (SVP International). As an intrapreneurial executive he was involved in forming the Squibb Hospital Division and Siemens Ultrasound and Nuclear Medicine Division. As an entrepreneurial executive he started corporations in the areas of clinical chemistry (Vice President of Marketing at IRIS), dermatology lasers (CEO of Innovative Health Concepts), orthopedic implants (CEO of the Kinamed division of Kyocera), and long-term and post-acute care (LTPAC) software (Vice President of Business Development and Marketing for Shared Healthcare Systems).

Since 2002 he has been directly involved with LTPAC, having been Executive Vice-President (EVP) of the American Health Care Association, representing skilled nursing facilities and assisted living facilities, and Senior Vice-President (SVP) Chief Information Officer (CIO) for Golden Living LLC, a major long-term care provider with over 300 facilities. He is and has been a member of various federal and corporate advisory boards as well as an advisor on grants in clinical technology, medication management, and health information exchanges. He was appointed to the Federal Advisory Committee on Standards, established by the Health & Human Services (HHS) Office of the National Coordinator for Health Information Technology's (ONC) Health Information Technology for Economic and Clinical Health (HITECH) Act in 2009, and served for seven years representing LTPAC. He has been a member of numerous committees and taskforces representing LTPAC as well as representing LTPAC on the Certificate Commission for Healthcare Information Technology's (CCHIT) Board of Trustees. He served on the Veterans' Affairs (VA) Congressional Oversight Committees in the areas of prosthetics/special devices and geriatrics. He is a member of the Healthcare Information and Management Systems Society's (HIMSS) Connected Health Committee and Co-Chair of the HIMSS LTPAC Roundtable.

He is one of the three founders of the LTPAC Health IT Collaborative after, in 2004, the Secretary of the HHS, Tommy George Thompson, asked Derr to coordinate the LTPAC Health IT (HIT) Summit. He is a retired U.S. Navy Captain of the Line, having served 31 years in the Navy both on active duty and in the active Naval Reserve. He served as the Reserve Commanding Officer of two USS Destroyers as well as other naval commands. He was awarded the Navy Meritorious Service Medal in 1989. He is a 2006 Distinguished Alumnus of Purdue University, where he received his bachelor degree in pharmacy in 1958.

 **Mr. Lorren Pettit (MS, MBA)** has been a healthcare researcher and strategist for more than twenty-five years, with experience in healthcare operations, corporate planning, and organizational development. Lorren began his hospital career leading the Geriatric Behavioral Health program for All Saints Health System (Fort Worth, TX). During his tenure with All Saints, he earned his nursing home administrator's license before moving into the health system's strategic planning department. Mr. Pettit transitioned into the hospital alliance/supply chain world with VHA Inc., where he led research/strategic planning activities,

before moving into the healthcare patient/provider satisfaction consulting industry with Press Ganey Associates.

He completed his undergraduate work at the University of Winnipeg (Winnipeg, Manitoba, Canada), and achieved a master of science in gerontology from Baylor University (Waco, TX) and a master of business administration from the University of Dallas, Texas. Mr. Pettit served for a number of years as an adjunct faculty member at Indiana University teaching medical sociology, social marketing, and gerontology.

Currently, Mr. Pettit is Vice President for HIS and Research for HIMSS. In his current role, Lorren has oversight of four key HIMSS initiatives:

1. HIMSS-sponsored thought leadership research
2. Advancing HIMSS's support of long-term/post-acute care (LTPAC) and behavioral health (BH) information and technology interests
3. Provider use of connected health technologies
4. HIMSS's support of Canadian Digital Health communities

Mr. Pettit resides in the Nashville, Tennessee, area with his wife, two boys, and baby girl.

Introduction

"Good Morning!" said Bilbo, and he meant it. The sun was shining, and the grass was very green. But Gandalf looked at him from under long bushy eyebrows that stuck out further than the brim of his shady hat.

"What do you mean?" he said. "Do you wish me a good morning, or mean that it is a good morning whether I want it or not; or that you feel good this morning; or that it is a morning to be good on?"

"All of them at once," said Bilbo.

J.R.R. Tolkien
The Hobbit

The task of writing an introductory textbook about information technology in the long-term/post-acute provider setting is much harder than one might think. It is not that the subject is complex or the concepts impossible to grasp; the challenge, like Bilbo's "good morning" salutation, is that the terms "long-term/post-acute care" (LTPAC) and "information technology" (IT) can mean different things to different people. Gaining consensus around what type of healthcare organizations fall under the umbrella of LTPAC and what type of technologies are part of a clinical electronic health record (EHR) system can be trying to say the least.

Yet, the need for a basic primer surrounding IT in LTPAC environments is perhaps greater now than ever before. A multiplicity of factors during the past number of years has been placing pressure on provider organizations from across the healthcare ecosystem to ensure they have the capabilities to "play in the electronic patient data sandbox" with other healthcare provider organizations. While LTPAC provider organizations have long played a significant role in the healthcare delivery system, the demands to integrate with LTPAC provider organizations have intensified. As a result, LTPAC provider organizations are working to expand their capabilities and use of health IT systems.

A significant challenge facing LTPAC provider organizations as they advance their IT systems involves workforce issues. Simply stated, for an IT system to be successful in an organization, the system needs a professional IT workforce. Unfortunately, due to a myriad of factors, there is a shortage of IT workers to support this growing sector of the healthcare ecosystem. The lack of a robust workforce is disconcerting as it presents a significant potential "bottleneck" in the integration of LTPAC provider organizations with other healthcare providers. Recognizing these workforce challenges, the present authors were inspired to develop a textbook to offer LTPAC workers, IT professionals, and those desiring to work in both of these areas with an introductory profile of key health IT topics as they apply to the LTPAC setting. Loosely following the array of topics Certified Professional in Health Information and Management Systems (CPHIMS) awardees must master, this textbook provides a foundation upon which LTPAC provider organizations can advance their IT capabilities.

The textbook is divided into four sections, with the first three reflecting CPHIMS-related material. The opening section of the textbook focuses on the *General Environment* within which LTPAC provider organizations and healthcare IT professionals operate. Chapter 1 purposes to bring some clarity to what is a complex and confusing U.S. healthcare landscape by dividing healthcare into four parts: Patients/Consumers; U.S. Payers and Providers; Oversight; and Technology and Infrastructure. Historically treated as secondary to the other players in the environment, Chapter 1 begins by discussing the elevated role patient/consumer interests are assuming in the delivery of care. The discussion then turns to the most complex part of the ecosystem to detail: U.S. Payers and Providers. Here, five major players falling under the U.S. Payers and Providers banner are identified and defined: payers, healthcare providers, healthcare provider organizations, ancillary medical services, and alternative payment models. LTPAC provider organizations, a subset of healthcare provider organizations, differentiate from one another by the dependency needs of the care recipient and the institutional nature of the site of care. The chapter closes by considering the oversight of the delivery of healthcare to include a brief review of the laws and regulations having the most disruptive effect on the advancement of health IT within the LTPAC environment. Chapter 2 continues a review of the U.S. healthcare landscape by addressing the fourth part of the ecosystem: the technological environment.

Section II of the textbook, *Systems*, concentrates on the activities LTPAC provider organizations should consider in selecting, implementing, and using health IT within their settings. This section opens by detailing the health IT life cycle within LTPAC settings. Parsed into two chapters, Chapter 3 focuses on the decision, selection, and acquisition activities of the health IT life cycle, whereas Chapter 4 concentrates on the life cycle's project management activities. Chapter 4 presents project management in three distinctive phases: Pre-Implementation, Implementation, and Post-Implementation. This section concludes by addressing the issues of privacy and security in Chapter 5. As an increasing number of LTPAC provider organizations use information technologies to manage patient data, the challenge of ensuring data privacy and security grows exponentially harder. Privacy and security is an area where IT leaders do not have the luxury of "on-the-job training."

The third section, *Administration*, addresses the all-important areas of IT leadership and management. Due to limited funds and resources, LTPAC provider organizations often lack on-site IT support services. Faced with a myriad of unique operational and organizational challenges, Chapter 6 reviews the demands LTPAC leaders and managers need to master in order to be effective in their organization.

The fourth and final section, *Other Considerations*, addresses the potential future for health IT within LTPAC settings (Chapter 7) before concluding with a review of health IT activities outside the United States in Chapter 8. While these latter two chapters are not topics typically covered in CPHIMS materials, the issues challenge LTPAC IT professionals to think critically and be more like Frodo Baggins; to look outside the realm of what is known and comfortable.

GENERAL
ENVIRONMENT

Chapter 1

LTPAC and the Healthcare Environment

Learning Objectives

Reading this chapter will help you to

- Identify four major parts of the healthcare ecosystem.
- List seven different categories of patients/consumers.
- Describe the characteristics and services of different types of healthcare provider organizations.
- Explain the disruptive influence various policy factors have had on the advancement of health IT in LTPAC provider organizations.

Introduction

Simply stated, the U.S. healthcare landscape is complex and confusing. This situation derives from, among other things, a landscape influenced by complex social and political forces, shrinking reimbursements, persistent shortages of health professionals, endless requirements to use performance and safety indicators, and prevailing calls for transparency. To navigate successfully within this environment, healthcare workers regardless of where they work within the industry need to have a competency surrounding their knowledge of the healthcare system.

The need for enhanced environmental awareness is especially true for those overseeing health information technology (IT) within the long-term/post-acute care (LTPAC) industry. Long treated as marginal players within the healthcare ecosystem, healthcare organizations across the spectrum are beginning to reconsider their data exchange relationships with LTPAC provider organizations. This renewed interest stems in part from the ecosystem's current trend to focus on things that have the greatest overall impact on the health of targeted populations, as well as the pressure to find ways to optimize health outcomes at an affordable cost. For those involved in the IT profession within LTPAC settings, understanding the healthcare ecosystem is important because it provides the macroeconomic context within which health information managers and technologists perform their art. The health information manager and technologist ensure that the best possible information management and systems support are available to improve the quality of life for the greatest number of individuals covered in the population under the provider's care.

There are a multiplicity of ways to bring the complexity of the U.S. healthcare system into focus. The approach in this textbook has been to divide the healthcare ecosystem into the following parts:

1. Patients/Consumers
2. U.S. Payers and Providers
3. Oversight
4. Technology and Infrastructure

This chapter addresses the first three of these components, with the Technology and Infrastructure discussion reserved for Chapter 2.

Patients/Consumers

It is appropriate to begin a conversation about the healthcare ecosystem with Patients/Consumers because these individuals should be at the center of the healthcare ecosystem. The organization of the current healthcare ecosystem primarily reflects the provider's perspective. It attempts to balance what providers have thought is best for patients with the provider's personal interests. Patients in this atmosphere are passive objects. This mindset is changing though with the advent of the person-centered electronic longitudinal care movement. With this movement, the person-centered perspective takes a much more active, prominent role working as partners with healthcare professionals in guiding clinical treatment decisions and optimizing one's health (NEJM Catalyst, 2017). The person-centered electronic longitudinal care movement recognizes the complexity and uniqueness of patients/consumers and aligns with efforts to personalize medicine (Personalized Medicine Coalition, n.d.).

Accompanying the move to elevate the individualistic nature of patient–clinician interactions are efforts to categorize like types of patients/consumers. Long used in other industries, a growing number of healthcare organizations are applying market segmentation techniques to their population health efforts in order to gain "economies of scale." Market segmentation is the process of dividing a broad population into subgroups based on some type of shared characteristics. The methods used to divide patient population groups can range from the simplistic (e.g. segmenting by age or gender) to the advanced use of statistical computation programs (e.g. cluster analysis). There is no universally accepted segmentation of persons/consumers with a myriad of approaches designed to achieve varied purposes. The most obvious approach is to leverage demographic dimensions such as gender, age, race, etc. Although these dimensions are important, they usually provide little understanding about how and why persons/consumers go about selecting and using healthcare services.

A more sophisticated person/consumer segmentation approach is to analyze past "purchase" (aka *person encounter*) data (from an organization's electronic health record (EHR) system and billing system) with known external behavior, consumer, and geospatial data. Carolinas HealthCare System (CHS), a large healthcare provider organization operating throughout North and South Carolina, employed such an approach using data from their 2.2 million patients (Butcher, 2016). By using a sophisticated hierarchical cluster analysis, CHS's patients sorted into seven mutually exclusive groups, with the following six groups clustering together because of traits they tended to share:

1. *Advanced cancer*: Persons with high-resource utilization and cancer diagnoses.
2. *Complex chronic*: Older, low-income, persons covered by Medicare, widowed, struggling with behavioral health problems and multiple chronic conditions.
3. *Aging rising risk*: Married, commercially insured persons with just one chronic condition (e.g. Type 2 diabetes) that was under control.
4. *Mental health*: Older teen/young adult males who have serious mental health conditions that require a great deal of support.
5. *Pregnancies and deliveries*: Healthy pregnant women.
6. *Newborns and toddlers*: Healthy children under age three.

Of particular interest to LTPAC workers is the use of segmentation efforts to differentiate seniors by their care needs. Kaiser Permanente (KP), a large multistate health plan and provider organization, developed a senior segmentation model using a combination of risk scores and clinical criteria (Zhou, Wong, & Li, 2014). Referred to as the *Senior Segmentation Algorithm*, this tool categorizes seniors into one of the following four population care groups:

1. *Care group 1*: Robust seniors without chronic conditions.
2. *Care group 2*: Seniors with one or more chronic conditions, such as diabetes, heart disease, and depression.
3. *Care group 3*: Seniors with advanced illness and end-organ failure, such as heart failure or chronic obstructive pulmonary disease.
4. *Care group 4*: Seniors with advanced frailty or at the end of life.

Though individuals move between care groups over time, this tool allows organizations to develop interventions and programs designed to meet a person's distinct needs within each care group.

The priority of persons/consumers in the healthcare ecosystem is of special interest to health IT professionals in LTPAC settings because consumers are increasingly requesting electronic versions of their charts from their providers. In fact, many EHR systems now offer patient portals permitting patients to view test results (after the provider's review and release of these to the patient), ask for prescription refills, and send the provider or the office staff an e-mail as well as schedule an appointment. The demand for LTPAC provider organizations to offer electronic access portals should grow exponentially as a growing number of family members and friends assume increasingly greater responsibility for an aging person's treatment decisions and care. Patient portals and other health IT solutions offer family caregivers a means to manage the stressors of looking after an aging person.

U.S. Payers and Providers

The U.S. Payers and Providers component of the healthcare ecosystem is by far the most complex part of the ecosystem to detail, in part because the landscape is constantly evolving. To simplify this topic, the following section will categorize this landscape as seen through the eyes of the person when accessing care. As such, the divisions in this market include:

1. Payers
2. Healthcare Providers
3. Healthcare Provider Organizations
4. Ancillary Medical Services
5. Alternative Payment Models

Payers

An entity that pays for or underwrites coverage for healthcare expenses. Payments generally come from three types of sources:

1. Government
2. Private insurance
3. Personal funds

1. *Government*: Government-financed and managed insurance programs are generally funded through taxes. These programs may pay for the healthcare system directly (e.g. the Veterans Administration), or provide funding for a national health insurance program (e.g. Medicare, Medicaid).
2. *Private insurance*: Insurance programs administered by private entities generally funded by employers, citizens, or a combination of both. The six most common types of health insurance plans are:
   a. *Health maintenance organizations (HMOs)*: A type of health insurance plan that usually limits coverage to care from doctors who work for or contract with the HMO. It generally will not cover out-of-network care except in an emergency. An HMO may require the insured to live or work in its service area to be eligible for coverage.

HMOs often provide integrated care and focus on prevention and wellness (HealthCare.gov, 2017a).

b. *Participating provider options (PPOs)*: A type of health plan where the insured pay less if they use providers in the plan's network. The insured can use doctors, hospitals, and providers outside of the network without a referral for an additional cost (HealthCare.gov, 2017b).

c. *Point-of-service (POS)*: This is a managed care plan that combines the features of HMOs and PPOs. These plans allow the insured to use a primary care physician (PCP) to coordinate their care, or they can self-direct their care at the point-of-service. The insured pay less if they use doctors, hospitals, and other healthcare providers that belong to the plan's network. POS plans require the insured to get a referral from their primary care doctor in order to see a specialist.

d. *Fee for service plans (indemnity)*: An insurance plan set up to reimburse medical providers for each "covered" service the insured receives on a case-by-case basis.

e. *Health savings accounts*: A type of medical savings account that allows individuals to save money to pay for current and future medical expenses on a tax-free basis.

3. *Personal funds*: People frequently use their own personal resources to fund all or part of their healthcare services, albeit because individuals do not have insurance coverage at all (whether by choice or because of financial constraints), or are paying for an insurance co-payment. In the United States, co-payments are required under most healthcare programs, whether government or privately managed.

Healthcare Providers

A healthcare provider is "an individual who provides preventive, curative, promotional or rehabilitative health care services in a systematic way to people, families or communities"

(Wikipedia, 2017). This definition covers a wide array of health professionals to include doctors of medicine or osteopathy, podiatrists, dentists, chiropractors, clinical psychologists, optometrists, nurse practitioners, nurse-midwives, nurses, and clinical social workers who are authorized to practice by the State and perform within the scope of their practice as defined by State law, as well as Christian Science practitioners.

One class of people most LTPAC provider organizations encounter, *family caregivers*, presents an interesting dilemma in relation to the classification of a healthcare provider. Given that family caregivers often look after the physical, emotional, and often financial support of another person who is unable to care for him/herself due to illness, injury, or disability, do they qualify as a healthcare provider? Are their services eligible for reimbursement? The short answer is that the affirmative is true "in some cases and some places." The chances of family members being paid for caregiving services are best if the individual being cared for is a U.S. military veteran or is eligible for Medicaid and lives in a state with a Medicaid care program (e.g. AARP, n.d.).

Healthcare Provider Organizations

A healthcare provider organization refers to a social unit of people structured and managed to deliver healthcare services through a specific care site to meet the health needs of varied populations. Healthcare provider organizations can manifest in a number of ways. Though not exhaustive, the present section will consider the following four types of provider organizations:

1. Hospitals
2. Outpatient or ambulatory care
3. Community health organizations
4. Long-term/post-acute care (LTPAC)

1. *Hospitals*: A hospital is a healthcare institution where clinical professionals treat the intensive health management needs of patients. Hospital categorizations are numerous and not always mutually exclusive. The following are the most common ways hospitals may be categorized:

   a. *Ownership type*: Refers to the business model guiding the organization's operational decisions.
      - *Public* or *government-managed hospitals* are hospitals owned by a government or governmental agency and receive government funding.
      - *Private hospitals* can be owned by a for-profit company (also referred to as *investor-owned hospitals*) or a nonprofit organization, allowing these type of organizations the advantage of avoiding taxes.

   b. *Service type*: The majority of U.S. hospitals are *general medical and surgical* hospitals supporting the most common types of medical and surgical care requirements. Hospitals specializing in more focused areas of care, such as *psychiatric* hospitals (which focus on mental and behavioral healthcare), *rehabilitation* hospitals (which focus on restoring neurological and musculoskeletal functions), and *children's* hospitals (which focus on the care and treatment of children), are becoming more prevalent in the United States.

   c. *Teaching status*: *Teaching* hospitals train future physicians and other healthcare providers. These types of hospitals are often associated with academic institutions or universities. A subset of teaching hospitals, *academic medical centers* (AMCs) or *university* hospitals contribute substantially to medical research and publish much of the knowledge that advances the science of medicine.

   d. *Location*: Hospital location (*urban* hospitals vs. *rural* hospitals) plays a factor in hospital categorization as it relates to challenges in accessing various resources. Small community hospitals located in rural areas of the United States may apply for designation as critical access hospitals (CAH), allowing them to receive higher reimbursement rates.

2. *Outpatient or ambulatory care*: Patient care not requiring the intensive management of a hospital setting is available in less "acute" outpatient or ambulatory care settings, such as a physician's office. There are a multiplicity of outpatient or ambulatory care settings, to include *single independent provider offices, large multiprovider group practices* in which a wide range of specialists may be available, *ambulatory surgery centers* or *surgi-centers*, and even *hospital emergency departments*.

3. *Community health organizations*: In the United States, community health organizations or centers are community-based and patient-directed organizations funded by federal grants that endeavor to provide "comprehensive, culturally competent, high-quality primary health care services" to medically underserved communities and vulnerable populations (Health Resources and Services Administration, n.d.).

4. *Long-term/post-acute care (LTPAC)*: The term LTPAC is difficult to define because it has come to mean so many different things to different people. Gaining consensus around what type of healthcare organizations fall under the umbrella of LTPAC can be trying, to say the least. Yet it is still incumbent upon the present authors to provide the reader clarity around the use of the term in this textbook. Therefore, unless otherwise noted, LTPAC refers to *specific healthcare provider organizations focused on the provision of care to individuals who have some degree of extended care dependency needs*. The organizations falling under the LTPAC banner in this book are:

   a. *Assisted living facilities (ALF)*: A type of residential long-term care setting offering a combination of personalized supportive services and healthcare designed to meet the needs, both scheduled and unscheduled, of those who need help with the activities of daily living.

b. *Continuous care retirement communities (CCRC)*: Also known as *planned living communities* (PLC), these are a type of residential long-term care setting offering residents a continuum of care ranging from independent living through assisted living, and ultimately nursing home care.

c. *Home health agencies (HHA)*: An organization that is primarily engaged in providing skilled nursing services and other therapeutic services in the patient's residence.

d. *Hospice centers*: Healthcare provider organizations focused on caring, not curing. The delivery of hospice care can occur in a number of settings ranging from the patient's home, freestanding hospice centers, hospitals, nursing homes, and other long-term care facilities.

e. *Independent rehabilitation facilities (IRF)*: An organization devoted to the rehabilitation of patients with various neurological, musculoskeletal, orthopedic, and other medical conditions following the stabilization of an acute medical issue. Rehabilitation hospitals provide less costly care than general hospitals while providing a higher level of professional therapies such as speech therapy, occupational therapy, and physical therapy than those available in skilled nursing care facilities.

f. *Skilled/nursing facilities (SNF)*: Nursing homes, now more commonly known as *skilled nursing facilities* (SNFs), serve as licensed healthcare residences for individuals who require a higher level of medical care than can be provided in an assisted living facility. Skilled nursing facilities may house short-term residents, typically for less than 30 days for rehabilitation, or long-term residents, who are typically there for longer than 30 days and extending up to several years.

g. *Long-term acute care hospitals (LTACH)*: LTACHs provide extended medical and rehabilitative care to individuals with clinically complex problems (e.g. mechanical ventilator weaning, administration of intravenous antibiotics, and complex wound care) needing hospital-level care for relatively extended periods. To qualify as an LTACH for Medicare payment, a facility must meet Medicare's conditions of participation for acute-care hospitals and have an average inpatient length of stay greater than 25 days (Weinstein & Munoz-Price, 2009).

Arguably, there are two main factors differentiating the LTPAC organizations just listed: (1) the extent to which the organization supports the care *dependency* needs of the person/resident and (2) the *institutional* nature of the care setting (low institutionalization = home-like environments; high institutionalization = medically intensive environments). When plotted on an x–y graph, the LTPAC ecosystem resembles Figure 1.1.

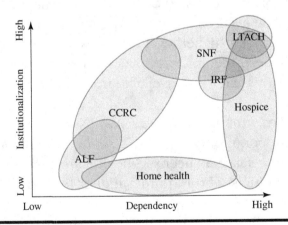

Figure 1.1   The LTPAC ecosystem.

Ancillary Medical Services

Ancillary medical services such as diagnostic services and pharmaceutical treatments can play a critical role in an effective healthcare intervention. While larger hospitals will generally have these capabilities, smaller hospitals, outpatient care centers, community health organizations, and LTPAC provider organizations will usually rely upon external providers to provide these supportive services to their patients. Key services provided in this area include laboratory, anatomic and anatomical pathology, diagnostic imaging and radiology, and pharmaceutical services.

Alternative Payment Models (APMs)

Historically, the U.S. healthcare system operated via a "fee-for-service" payment model where healthcare provider reimbursement reflected the *volume* rather than the *value* of the services offered. In recent years, there has been a shift towards value-based payment schemas. An alternative payment model (APM) is a payment approach that rewards providers for delivering high-quality and cost-efficient care. APMs are included in the *U.S. Payers and Providers* section because APM models like accountable care organizations (ACOs) and person-centered medical homes are emerging players in the healthcare ecosystem landscape. These types of organizations pull many of the previously cited payers and providers together in order to focus on coordinated, team-based care and improved outcomes.

Before moving on to the third component of the healthcare ecosystem, it is important to recognize that the disparate provider organizations discussed here do not operate independently of one another. There are many reasons for the interrelationships among the various players. These include enabling comprehensive care, ensuring effective transfers of care, ensuring the general portability of information in support of care, reporting public and population health information, obtaining appropriate reimbursement for care, and supporting particular organizational models of care. Most times when a provider or provider organization determines a patient's scope of care is outside one's capability, the care transfers to another provider or healthcare organization. This transfer is significant to the LTPAC health IT professional because it involves the creation of a Continuity of Care Document (CCD). The CCD is a document summarizing the most commonly needed pertinent information about a patient's/resident's current and past health statuses. Using Composite Clinical Document Architecture (C-CDA) standards, this information is exchangeable electronically in a format shared by all computer applications. The electronic exchange of a care document is vital as clinical staff implement a plan of care and coordinate services across disparate organizations. Six non-emergent use cases for planning care and coordinating services communicated by nursing facility staff are: (1) scheduling appointments, (2) laboratory specimen drawing, (3) pharmacy orders and reconciliation, (4) social work discharge planning, (5) admissions and pre-admissions, and (6) pharmacy-medication reconciliation (Alexander, et al., 2015). Obviously, the effective communication of health information becomes exceptionally important to the person's welfare during the transfer of care. This is the special role health information and technology plays in ensuring the correct health information is available when clinicians need it.

Oversight

A third component of the healthcare ecosystem involves those entities and efforts involved in the oversight of the delivery of healthcare services:

1. Laws and Regulations
2. Regulatory Bodies

Laws and Regulations

Regulation plays a major role in the healthcare industry and healthcare insurance coverage. Healthcare regulations are developed and implemented not only by all levels of government organization (federal, state, and local) but by private organizations as well. Healthcare regulations and standards are necessary to ensure compliance and to provide safe healthcare to every individual who accesses the system. Perhaps the two most significant laws and regulations to have affected healthcare information and technology in the current ecosystem are:

1. *HIPAA Privacy Rule (HIPAA)*: The Health Insurance Portability and Accountability Act of 1996 (HIPAA) established a national standard to protect a patient's medical record and other personal health information. HIPAA requires appropriate safeguards to protect the privacy of personal health information, and sets limits and conditions on the uses and disclosures of the information without patient authorization. The rule also gives patients rights over their health information, including rights to examine and obtain a copy of their health records, and to request corrections.
2. *Health Information Technology for Economic and Clinical Health (HITECH) Act*: The 2009 HITECH Act established programs to improve healthcare quality, safety, and efficiency by using health IT, including EHRs and private and secure electronic health information exchanges.

Arguably, laws and regulations have played a significant role in advancing digital health innovations within the LTPAC marketplace too. While it is not in the scope of this textbook to provide an exhaustive review of legislative and regulatory impacts on the LTPAC provider community, the following briefly summarizes some of the legislation resulting in the most disruptive changes in the LTPAC landscape.

1. *Omnibus Budget Reconciliation Act of 1987 (OBRA '87)*: The Nursing Home Reform Act contained in OBRA '87 was a federal law requiring the states and federal government to inspect nursing homes on a regular basis, and to enforce standards by using a range of sanctions (USLegal, n.d.). The law also required nursing home providers to provide SNF residents with regular evaluations of their activities of daily living (ADL), resulting in the implementation of the national nursing home Resident Assessment Instrument (RAI). This provision was disruptively significant because the federal government introduced the idea of the electronic collection and submission of patient data into the nursing home environment.

2. *Balanced Budget Act (BBA) of 1997*: The Balanced Budget Act of 1997 (BBA) was aimed at reducing national Medicare costs by $116.4 billion over a five-year period (1998–2002) (The Commonwealth Fund, n.d.). It created a new prospective payment system (PPS) and instituted other changes that substantially affected reimbursement, billing, administration, and staffing in provider organizations to include hospitals, home health agencies, and skilled nursing facilities. This law was disruptive for nursing home providers in that it elevated the importance of electronic patient data via the establishment of the Minimum Data Set (MDS) electronic assessment. To be reimbursed for the care they provided, SNFs would need to electronically submit MDS data to the federal government via a payment software program (Raven) provided by *the* Centers for Medicare and Medicaid Services (CMS) (CMS, n.d.). This development in effect steered the use of computers in nursing homes (and eventually HHAs, IRFs, and LTACHs) towards managing the financial aspects of resident/person care versus the clinical uses of the technology.

3. *President Bush's Executive Order (EO) 13335 of April 2004*: President Bush's April 27, 2004 Executive Order marked a significant moment in the evolution of health information and technology in the U.S. healthcare system. By establishing the Office of the National Coordinator for Health Information Technology (ONC) within the Office of the Secretary of Health and Human Services (HHS), the federal government took a huge step towards actualizing its vision for a national health IT architecture (ONC, 2008). The focus of ONC on hospitals and physicians encouraged LTPAC health IT leaders to organize and advance their collective interests.

4. *American Recovery and Reinvestment (ARRA) Act and Health Information Technology for Economic and Clinical Health (HITECH) Act of 2009*: The HITECH Act, enacted as part of the ARRA, promoted the adoption and meaningful use (MU) of health information technology through incentive funds for qualified acute care hospitals and ambulatory physicians. The omission of LTPAC providers from the MU incentive program was disruptively significant in that it has arguably accelerated the digital divide between LTPAC providers and MU eligible providers.

5. *Improving Medicare Post-Acute Care Transformation (IMPACT) Act of 2014*: The IMPACT Act requires LTACHs, SNFs, HHAs, and IRFs to report CMS-standardized assessment data elements in certain quality measure domains, and requires CMS to make assessment data elements interoperable. This latter point was significant to advancing the use of health IT in LTPAC settings because CMS was obligated to make data elements interoperable by linking the elements to health IT standards (Harvell, O'Malley, & Palena Hall, 2016).

6. *Medicare Access and CHIP Reauthorization Act of 2015 (MACRA)*: This Act is an example of a legislative and regulatory issue that does not specifically address the use of health IT LTPAC settings, but has implications for these

provider organizations nonetheless. In this Act, physicians participating in the Merit-Based Incentive Payment System (MIPS) are mandated to use a certified interoperable and electronic standard Continuity of Care Document (CCD or C-CDA) when transitioning the care of patients to other providers. By extension, LTPAC organizations are impacted by this Act as physicians (geriatricians SNF medical directors, and advanced practice nurses) working with LTPAC organizations are required to have a current health IT software enterprise system.

7. *21st Century Cures Act of 2016*: This Act promotes and funds the acceleration of research into preventing and curing serious illnesses; accelerates drug and medical device development; attempts to address the opioid abuse crisis; and tries to improve mental health-service delivery.

8. *2018 proposed revised payment system and change of the RUG system*: As this textbook goes to print, CMS is proposing a new Medicare payment system for SNFs, called the Resident Classification System, Version I (RCS-I). The new reimbursement system aims to (1) more accurately compensate SNFs; (2) reduce incentives for SNFs to deliver therapy based on financial considerations, rather than resident need; and (3) maintain simplicity, to the extent possible. While the specifics and exact implications of the law are not clear at this time, the reader should be aware of these proposed changes.

Regulatory Bodies

Various health regulatory bodies protect the public from a number of health risks and provide numerous programs for public health and welfare. The healthcare regulatory agencies in turn monitor practitioners and provider organizations, provide information about industry changes, promote safety, and ensure legal compliance and quality services. The following are agencies and regulatory bodies, all within the U.S. Department of Health and Human Services (HHS), that most closely govern the use of health IT through the law and by functioning as healthcare compliance resources (TechTarget, n.d.):

1. *The Office for Civil Rights (OCR)*: The OCR is responsible for enforcing HIPAA privacy and security rules by investigating privacy violations and enforcing penalties for noncompliance.
2. *The Centers for Medicare and Medicaid Services (CMS)*: CMS oversees most of the regulations related directly to the healthcare system. CMS is responsible for the administration of the following government-subsidized medical coverage programs:
   a. *Medicare*: Health insurance program for the elderly and disabled
   b. *Medicaid*: Health insurance program for lower-income individuals and families
   c. *Children's Health Insurance Program (CHIP)*: Health insurance program for children under 19

   The HITECH Act added several key tasks to CMS's list of responsibilities, intended to advance the meaningful use of health IT in provider organizations.
3. *The Office of the National Coordinator for Health IT (ONC)*: ONC is the principal entity responsible for coordinating nationwide efforts to implement and use advanced health information technology and health information exchange. ONC's mission includes coordinating health IT policy, providing leadership in the development, recognition, and implementation of standards, and the certification of health IT products.
4. *The Agency for Healthcare Research and Quality (AHRQ)*: The AHRQ is an agency that conducts research aimed at improving the quality of healthcare, reducing costs, and addressing patient safety and medical errors. AHRQ has a long history of funding research in LTPAC settings with a focus on health IT.

5. *The U.S. Food and Drug Administration (FDA)*: Congress first gave the FDA complete authority over medical devices in the Food, Drug, and Cosmetic Act of 1938. During the late 1970s medical device amendments targeted issues of patient access and patient safety and marshaled in new innovations in health IT. Current earmarks for regulating medical devices include new models to generate evidence through a National Evaluation System for health Technology (NEST) to ensure access and safety of patients in every type of healthcare system (FDA, 2016).
6. *The Occupational Safety and Health Administration (OSHA)*: This agency oversees many labor-force safety issues, including hazardous material and lifting.

Summary

The purpose of this chapter has been to bring some clarity to what is clearly a complex and confusing U.S. healthcare landscape. A critical issue to understand, health IT workers in LTPAC settings should be especially interested in this topic because it provides the macroeconomic context within which they perform. The approach used to describe the healthcare ecosystem was to divide healthcare players into four parts (Patients/Consumers; U.S. Payers and Providers; Oversight; Technology and Infrastructure), the first three being addressed in this chapter.

The first part of the healthcare environment considered purposely began with *patients and consumers*. Historically treated as secondary to the other players in the environment, there is a growing trend to ensure patient/consumer interests play a much more elevated role in the delivery of care.

The second part of the ecosystem addressed, *U.S. Payers and Providers*, is by far the most complex part of the ecosystem to detail. There are five major players falling under the U.S. Payers and Providers banner (payers; healthcare providers; healthcare provider organizations; ancillary medical services; alternative payment models). LTPAC provider organizations, a subset of healthcare provider organizations, can perhaps best be differentiated based on two factors: the dependency needs of the care recipient and the institutional nature of the site of care.

The third part of the healthcare environment covered involved the oversight of the delivery of healthcare. This section included a review of the laws and regulations having the most disruptive effects on the advancement of health IT within the LTPAC environment.

For Discussion

1. Discuss how understanding the healthcare ecosystem may help you in your career as a health IT professional.
2. Discuss the experiences of yourself or others as a person/ consumer.
3. Explain how LTPAC provider organizations use health IT to support family caregivers.
4. Compare and contrast the different types of healthcare provider organizations.
5. Identify the different types of LTPAC provider organizations operating within your community. Discuss your impression of these organizations.
6. Explain how policy factors have advanced the adoption of health IT in LTPAC provider organizations. Explain how policy factors may have hindered the advancement of health IT use in LTPAC provider organizations.

References

AARP. (n.d.). Can I Get Paid to Be a Caregiver For a Family Member? Retrieved from AARP: https://www.aarp.org/caregiving/financial-legal/info-2017/managing-money-loved-ones.html

Alexander, G. L., Rantz, M., Galambos, C., Vogelsmeier, A., Flesner, M., Popejoy, L., … Elvin, M. (2015). Preparing Nursing Homes for the Future of Health Information Exchange. *Applied Clinical Informatics*, April 15, 6(2), 248–266.

Butcher, L. (2016, March 8). Consumer Segmentation Has Hit Health Care. Here's How It Works. *Hospitals & Health Networks*.

CMS. (n.d.). Introduction to the Resident Assessment Validation and Entry (RAVEN) System Software. Retrieved from CMS: https://www.cms.gov/Research-Statistics-Data-and-Systems/ Computer-Data-and-Systems/MinimumDataSets20/Downloads/ RAVENSoftwareIntroduction.pdf

FDA. (2016). Food and Drug Administration (FDA) FDA Celebrates the 40th Anniversary of the Medical Device Amendments. Comments by Jeffery Shuren, June 22, 2016. Retrieved from FDA U.S. Food and Drug Administration: https://blogs.fda.gov/ fdavoice/index.php/tag/fdas-oversight-on-medical-devices/

Harvell, J., O'Malley, T. A., & Palena Hall, E. (2016, February 4). IMPACT Act: Connecting Post-Acute Care Across the Care Continuum. Retrieved from Medicare Learning Network: https://www.cms.gov/Outreach-and-Education/Outreach/NPC/ Downloads/2016-02-04-IMPACTAct-Presentation.pdf

Health Resources & Services Administration. (n.d.). What Is a Health Center? Retrieved from HRSA: Health Center Program: https:// bphc.hrsa.gov/about/what-is-a-health-center/index.html

HealthCare.gov. (2017). Glossary: Health Maintenance Organization (HMO). Retrieved from HealthCare.gov: https://www.healthcare. gov/glossary/health-maintenance-organization-HMO/

HealthCare.gov. (2017). Health Insurance Plan & Network Types: HMOs, PPOs, and More. Retrieved from HealthCare.gov: https:// www.healthcare.gov/choose-a-plan/plan-types/

NEJM Catalyst. (2017, January 1). What Is Patient-Centered Care? Retrieved from NEJM Catalyst: https://catalyst.nejm.org/ what-is-patient-centered-care/

ONC. (2008). *The ONC-Coordinated Federal Health Information Technology Strategic Plan: 2008–2012*. ONC.

Personalized Medicine Coalition. (n.d.). About PMC. Retrieved from Personalized Medicine Coalition: http://www.personalizedmedi- cinecoalition.org/About_Us/About_PMC

TechTarget. (n.d.). Guide to Healthcare Compliance Resources and Agencies. Retrieved from SearchHealthIT: http://searchhealthit.techtarget.com/essentialguide/Guide-to-healthcare-compliance-resources-and-agencies

The Commonwealth Fund. (n.d.). An Examination of Key Medicare Provisions in the Balanced Budget Act of 1997. Retrieved from The Commonwealth Fund: http://www.commonwealthfund.org/publications/fund-reports/1997/sep/an-examination-of-key-medicare-provisions-in-the-balanced-budget-act-of-1997

USLegal. (n.d.). Federal Nursing Home Reform Act (OBRA'87) Law and Legal Definition. Retrieved from USLegal: https://definitions.uslegal.com/f/federal-nursing-home-reform-act-obra-87/

Weinstein, R. A., & Munoz-Price, L. S. (2009). Long-Term Acute Care Hospitals. *Clinical Infectious Diseases*, August 1, 49(3), 438–443.

Wikipedia. (2017). Health Professional. Retrieved from Wikipedia: https://en.wikipedia.org/wiki/Health_professional

Zhou, Y., Wong, W., & Li, H. (2014). Improving Care for Older Adults: A Model to Segment the Senior Population. *The Permanente Journal*, Summer, 18(3), 18–21.

Chapter 2

LTPAC and the Technology Environment

Learning Objectives

Reading this chapter will help you to

- Articulate characteristics of technology infrastructure that support the healthcare environment (e.g. network, communications, data integration, privacy, and security).
- Articulate characteristics of applications commonly used in healthcare (e.g. clinical, administrative, and consumer information systems).

Introduction

The healthcare ecosystem as outlined in the previous chapter divides into four component parts. Whereas Chapter 1 addressed the first three of these parts (Patients/Consumers, U.S. Payers and Providers, and healthcare Oversight), this chapter focuses on the fourth component, Technology and Infrastructure. It is significant to devote an entire chapter to this fourth component because healthcare IT is radically changing the way provider organizations (to include LTPAC providers) interact with patients/consumers and facilitate the delivery of care.

Information systems allow for the creation, processing, storage, and dissemination of information to support decisions made by organizations and the people within them. Two broad components of the technology environment support the advances evidenced within the healthcare industry:

1. *Technology infrastructure*: Composed of *hardware* (which includes the servers, network connections, and devices used to access information), and *networks* (wired or wireless connections linking the infrastructure together enabling the accessibility of applications and patient data).
2. *Applications*: The software providers use to process and store data, manage patients' records and provide information.

The purpose of this chapter is to discuss the technology infrastructure that supports the healthcare provider marketplace as well as the applications commonly used by providers. The topics addressed will be conceptual in nature because of the constantly evolving technology infrastructure and applications landscape.

Before reviewing the varied components of the technology environment, it is helpful to have a framework for understanding how the technology infrastructure allows applications to communicate over a network. The Open Systems Interconnection (OSI) model of communication, developed by the International Standards Organization (ISO), is a frequently cited conceptual model for relating different technologies with one another (Wikipedia, n.d.). Referenced in vendor literature and many certification preparation materials, the OSI model is an important model for the health IT professional to understand.

At its core, the OSI model is a conceptual framework characterizing the standardized communication functions of a telecommunication or computing system regardless of the underlying internal structure and technology. The model partitions a communication system into seven "layers" with each layer serving the layer above it and being served by the layer below it. The layers are responsible for a set of functional tasks during data transmission and guided by a set of protocols. Table 2.1 summarizes the seven layers and their

Table 2.1   The Open Systems Interconnection (OSI) Telecommunications Model

Layer	Name	Role
7	Application	High-level application programming interfaces, including resource sharing and remote file access
6	Presentation	Translation of data between a networking service and an application; including character encoding, data compression, and encryption/decryption
5	Session	Managing communication sessions; i.e. the continuous exchange of information in the form of multiple back-and-forth transmissions between two nodes
4	Transport	Reliable transmission of data segments between points on a network, including segmentation, acknowledgment, and multiplexing
3	Network	Structuring and managing a multi-node network, including addressing, routing, and traffic control
2	Data link	Reliable transmission of data frames between two nodes connected by a physical layer
1	Physical	Transmission and reception of raw bit streams over a physical medium

functional roles. Upper layers of the model deal with network application programs and are usually implemented via software. Lower layers are responsible for data transmission and use both software and hardware.

Technology Infrastructure

Technology infrastructure refers to the hardware and network resources (as well as the services) required for the existence, operation, and management of an information system. The IT infrastructure consists of all of the components that play a role in overall IT and IT-enabled operations. A standard IT infrastructure consists of the following five components:

1. Data
2. Routers, Switches, and Servers
3. Wired and Wireless Networks
4. Client Terminals and Devices
5. Data Storage and Data Integration

Data

The technology infrastructure of an information system begins with, and centers on, data. As an OSI-model layer-1 function, data is information converted into a binary digital format that is efficient for processing or moving through a network. *Raw data* is a term used to describe data in its most basic digital format. There are a myriad of sources generating patient health information in a healthcare organization.

Routers, Switches, Servers

The routers, switches, and virtual and physical servers constitute some of the integral hardware parts needed to connect clinicians, administrators, providers, and patients to necessary business and clinical data. Though some tend to use the terms interchangeably, the functions of the three devices are quite different from one another, even if at times they integrate into a single device.

The *server* is an electronic device that provides functionality for other programs or devices, called "clients." A single server can serve multiple clients, and a single client can use multiple servers. Typical servers are database servers, file servers, mail servers, print servers, web servers, game servers, and application servers. Historically, servers have tended to be the most expensive equipment in a healthcare IT system. That said, *cloud computing*, a method for delivering information technology (IT) services by retrieving resources from the internet through web-based tools and applications as opposed to a direct connection to a server, may be changing this calculus. The *switch* is the electronic device that acts as a controller, enabling networked devices to talk to each other efficiently. Switches operate at layer 2 of the OSI model. The *router* is an electronic device that connects at least two computer networks together, most often two local area networks (LANs) or wide area networks (WANs), or a LAN and its internet service provider's (ISP) network. A router acts as a dispatcher of data packets, choosing the best path for information to travel. Routers operate at layer 3 of the OSI model.

Wired and Wireless Networks

An OSI-model layer-3 function, a network is a group of two or more computer systems linked together. There are many types of computer networks, with perhaps the two most common being local area networks (LANs: connected computers geographically close together such as in the same building; WLANs: wirelessly connected LANs) and wide area networks (WANs: geographically dispersed connected computers connected by telephone lines or radio waves). The following characteristics differentiate networks:

Topology: The geometric configuration of the computer system (e.g. star, ring).

Protocol: The common set of rules and signals that computers on the network use to communicate (e.g. Ethernet).

Architecture: The combination of hardware and/or software used in the network.

A network consists of both wireless and wired connections. While still dependent on network cables, an increasing number of healthcare organizations are using wireless connections.

Client Terminals and (Portable) Devices

The provision of care in healthcare organizations requires clinicians to be mobile. In fact, a study in 2003 found that hospital nurses in a medical-surgical unit walked an average of four to five miles during a 12-h shift (Welton, Decker, Adam, & Zone-Smith, 2006). Some of the distance nurses traveled undoubtedly involved treks to and from the point-of-care (e.g. patient's room) to a nurses' station to retrieve/enter clinical information. Client devices may be general-purpose devices such as PC terminals or smartphones, or dedicated devices such as medical equipment or building control systems. In many healthcare organizations, everything from the soda machine in the cafeteria to the building's security cameras, as well as bedside monitors, clinician workstations, and visitor smartphones may be connected. These numerous interconnected devices and systems increase the complexity, utility, and criticality of the network.

Portable devices such as smartphones and tablets, enabled by a wireless connected network, allow clinicians to access information at the point-of-care. A major concern with any handheld device that connects to the institution's network is security, especially when end users actually bring their own devices to work. Before allowing staff to use personal devices in clinical interventions, provider organizations need policies and protocols ensuring the privacy and security of patient data. While some portable devices can send and receive text messages, there are questions about the legality and safety of using text messages for patient orders. As these devices frequently traverse through patient care areas, infection control is a major concern. Materials for these devices need to be antibacterial and cleanable with harsh cleansing agents.

Data Storage and Data Integration

Data storage is a general term for archiving data in electro-magnetic or other forms for use by a computer or device. Data storage and retrieval is a significant issue in the health-care industry as regulations exist surrounding how long healthcare providers must maintain patient data. The length of time a provider is required to hold onto medical records varies by state. Maintained as a paper record, data storage can translate into a large expense in storing stacks of paper. Healthcare organizations use a multiplicity of electronic data storage formats to include magnetic tape, optical disc storage, hard drive storage, or cloud storage. *Data integration* and the use of interface engines are essential in healthcare information systems. It is not enough for organizations to send data from one application to another. If data does not go to the right patient's chart, errors in the patient's care, bill, and final report could result. Interface engines are tools that translate functions from different systems and protocols into a common format to facilitate information sharing. Without data integration and interface engines, a national health information network in either the United States or the rest of the world will never exist.

Applications

The highest level of the OSI model, layer 7, is the applications level. To many, software applications are the "face of health-care IT." Applications are software programs that provide some useful healthcare capability or functionality. These applications "sit" on top of the technological infrastructure or hardware of an information system and are the most visible parts of the IT system for most users.

Applications in healthcare IT generally fall into one of three areas:

1. Administrative Applications
2. Financial Applications
3. Clinical Applications

Administrative Applications

Administrative applications cover a wide array of administrative functions within a healthcare setting. These functions include electronic time cards, payroll, staff competency record keeping, and educational applications, as well as staff scheduling and scheduling for patient procedures and office visits. Bed management systems, which include staff from housekeeping and patient transportation as well as clinicians, are very helpful in getting patients into a room as soon as possible. Popular applications in the last few years include equipment tracking applications that use radio frequency identification technology, thus saving staff time spent hunting for needed equipment like wheelchairs.

The growing robustness of data in long-term care information systems is changing how provider organizations use administrative applications. The collection of longitudinal data (trending data over time) affords leaders the opportunity to develop predictive patient risk models allowing for optimal decision-making and early intervention. Some senior facilities even connect data systems to sensors in long-term care residents' apartments in order to monitor mobility patterns such as resident gait, gait speed, and stride length. When combined, these measures provide potent parameters to identify subtle changes in a resident's functional ability (Rantz, et al., 2017). Integrating these type of predictive clinical measures with administrative data (e.g. incidence of falls, frequency of hospitalizations or emergency room visits) provides insightful and actionable information that enhances business decisions and leads to better quality of care and reduced costs. Furthermore, these capabilities can have a positive impact on customer perceptions and their satisfaction with the care delivery systems.

Financial Applications

Healthcare financial applications address the financial aspects of a healthcare organization's operations. From the solo provider's office to the multi-provider health system, there is a need for robust financial systems. Healthcare financial management can be incredibly complex and professional associations like the Healthcare Financial Management Association (HFMA) exist to support those interested in developing their career within this side of the industry.

The categories of financial activities provider organizations need software programs to support are extensive and include:

Insurance: Insurance, coinsurance, and deductibles are key factors in a provider's reimbursement formula. Providers need software applications to manage revenue codes and supply items, and generate statements for patients and insurance companies as well as a host of other patient billing tasks.

General Ledger: A general ledger application tracks charges, bills, and payments.

Payroll: A payroll system takes labor hours data from the electronic time-card system and converts time into dollars

and cents, correctly matching hours worked, both regular
and overtime and calculating overtime bonuses, holiday
bonuses, shift differentials, and additional wages earned
from professional certifications. It also has to track earn-
ing for paid time off, usually based on the number of
hours worked by the employee.

Accounts payable (AP): AP software applications must be in
sync with all other systems to ensure the entire supply
chain process is correct.

Historically, financial management systems are more perva-
sive in LTPAC provider organizations than clinical information
systems. An understandable development, as LTPAC settings
first used electronic reporting for financial purposes. That said,
the percentage of U.S. skilled nursing facilities reported to be
using an electronic health record in 2016 was an impressive
64% (Ngafeeson, 2014).

As the healthcare system moves to a value-based risk-shar-
ing model, there will have to be more cost accounting done
on each patient in order to realize the true cost of care.

Clinical Applications

A clinical information system is a computer-based system
that uses clinical applications to assist providers in diagnos-
ing, treating, monitoring, and documenting patient care. Key
capabilities of IT systems in LTPAC have been identified in
resident care, clinical support, and administrative activities (see
Table 2.2) (Alexander and Wakefield, 2009). These key clinical
application capabilities have benefited the delivery of patient
care in the following ways:

1. *Supporting* patient care
2. *Transforming* patient care

Table 2.2 Draft Framework for Staging Domains of Healthcare and Attributes of IT Sophistication

Attributes of IT Sophistication	Domains of Healthcare		
	Resident care	*Clinical support*	*Administrative activities*
Health IT capabilities	Resident care activities supported by technology: • Admissions, discharges, transfers • Waiting list management • Bed availability estimation • Discharge summary • Order entry • Physician order sheet • Progress notes • Results reporting • Face sheet (abstracts)	Clinical processes supported by technology: • Staff scheduling • Vital signs recording • Medication admin. • Staff workload management. • Physician transcription • Care area assessment rapid assessment procedures (RAPS) • Historical records • Resident acuity • Quality assurance • Nursing flowsheet • Incident reporting • Real-time MDS/RAI • Clinical reporting • Label generation • Specimen archiving • Recurring tests management	Administrative activities supported by technology: • Tracking IT system issues • IT requests • IT "help desk" • Backup power source • Biotechnology • Resident ID • Electronic wand

(Continued)

Table 2.2 (Continued)   Draft Framework for Staging Domains of Healthcare and Attributes of IT Sophistication

Attributes of IT Sophistication	Domains of Healthcare		
	Resident care	Clinical support	Administrative activities
Extent of IT use	Technology used in resident care activities: • Electronic tracking, Medical records, Resident ID • Scanning medical records • Centralized scheduling • Dictation systems • Voice recognition systems • Connection to external databases • Expert system • Telemedicine • Access to radiological images • Analytics	Technology used in clinical support: • PCs at nursing station • PCs in the hallway • PCs on the medical cart • PCs at the bedside • Portable computing devices • Laptops • Handheld (PDA) • Touch screens	Technology used in administrative activities: • Databases • Networks • Operating systems • Fax machines • Fiber optics • Wide area network • Satellite connections • Microwave connections • Local area network • Integrated Service Delivery • Network (ISDN) • Wireless network • Modems • Infrared connections

(Continued)

Table 2.2 (Continued) Draft Framework for Staging Domains of Healthcare and Attributes of IT Sophistication

Attributes of IT Sophistication	Domains of Healthcare		
	Resident care	Clinical support	Administrative activities

Degree of IT integration	Degree of integration of resident care technology:
	
	• Resident management systems
	• Admissions
	• Scheduling resources availability
	• Laboratory
	• Pharmacy
	• Human resources
	• Finance
	• Medical/resident records
		Degree of integration of clinical support technology:
		
		• Electronic and automatic transfer of information between IT systems
		• Interoperability—ToC
		• Nursing IT integration
		  – Pharmacy
		  – Dietary
		  – physical therapy (PT)/ occupational therapy (OT)
		  – Laboratory
		• IT department
			Degree of integration of technology supporting administrative activities:
			
			• Environmental systems
			• Fire protection systems
			• Security access
			• Centralized systems
			• Disaster recovery plan
			• Nursing home website
			• External e-mail
			• Electronic bulletin boards
			• Intranet applications
			• Extranet applications
			• Enterprise resource planning

When discussing the clinical application's *support of patient care*, it is essential to first clarify the definitions of three commonly referenced types of clinical records used in the support of patient care: electronic health records (EHR), electronic medical records (EMR), and personal health records (PHR). All intimately tied to clinical applications, these records may seem interchangeable but actually have very different meanings.

> *EHR*: The EHR is a longitudinal electronic record of patient health information generated by one or more encounters in any care delivery setting. Included in the EHR is information about patients' demographics, progress notes, problems, medications, vital signs, past medical histories, immunizations, laboratory data, and radiology reports and images.
>
> *EMR*: Similar to the EHR, the EMR is a longitudinal electronic record confined to one specific setting.

> ■ *The terms EHR and EMR have also come to refer to an application environment composed of the clinical data repository, clinical decision support, controlled medical vocabulary, order entry, computerized practitioner order entry, and clinical documentation applications.*

> *PHR*: The PHR is a medical record often created, edited, maintained, and controlled by the patient. The electronic manifestation of this personal health record is an ePHR. PHRs fall under the consumer information systems rubric, which are hardware, software, and web-based applications designed to allow healthcare consumers to participate and manage their own healthcare via electronic resources (Agency for Healthcare Research and Quality (AHRQ), n.d.). Consumer health systems and clinical applications tend to be most successful when consumers are involved in all stages of the product development cycle. There are special considerations when considering design features for elderly end users such as security and

previous experiences with similar products (Czaja, Sharit, Nair, & Lee, 2008; Fisk, Rogers, Charness, Czaja, & Sharit, 2009). As an increased number of patients engage in their own healthcare and are empowered as vital members of their own care team, the PHR can expect to become a tool through which the caregiver can manage their health

The clinical application's support of patient care is most apparent in the EHR/EMR application environment where clinicians use these systems to do a whole host of patient care activities (e.g. retrieve patient data from a lab or pharmacy; document patient care; enter orders; send electronic prescriptions to the patient's pharmacy).

Clinical applications also *transform patient care*, especially with the availability of clinical data at the point-of-care. Physicians, for example, no longer need to go to the hospital's radiology department to look at MRIs or CT scans. Instead, they can access those images via the EHR/EMR saving time for clinicians as well as the organization's money.

An increasing number of LTPAC provider EMRs are gradually adding person-centric Clinical Decision Support (CDS) software into their systems. The CDS aggregates clinical data and applies analytics to the data to provide clinicians with clinical decision pathways. These analytics, mostly computed in the Cloud, promise to be very important in the treatment of chronic care patients with complex comorbidities. Advances in analytic software capabilities and new technologies like cognitive analytics and pharmacogenomics to fight polypharmacy are other capabilities that appear to have potential significant impact on the delivery of care in LTPAC settings.

Application Standards and Interoperability

Before leaving the topic of applications, it is essential to address the idea of *interoperability and standards*. Healthcare is too complex for a "one sizes fits all" approach. Healthcare systems require the use of a diverse array of software applications to work together (be "interoperable"). Interoperability, the extent to which systems and devices can exchange and interpret shared data, allows for the uniform movement of data from one system to another such that the clinical or operational purpose and meaning of the data are preserved and unaltered. Note that some clinicians prefer the term "transitions of care" (ToC) to the technological term "interoperability" as the former inherently recognizes the "human" aspect of the data exchanged.

The use of software standards (a standard, protocol, or other common format for a document, file, or data transfer accepted and used by one or more software developers while working on one, or more than one, computer programs), is critical to interoperability (Wikipedia, n.d.). Without standards, healthcare IT would most resemble the Tower of Babel, with no system or device speaking the same language and resulting in duplicative effort and work from clinical and administrative staff. Software standards enable interoperability between different programs created by different developers. With the current movement to exchanging patient data, regardless of the physical location of the patient and the patient's home data, those standards, especially for data formats and programming languages, have become increasingly important.

To be effective, interoperability must be timely. If a provider sends patient data to the EHR/EMR days after the patient enters the next provider site, the patient data becomes irrelevant. The new provider site has to conduct an assessment immediately upon receipt of the patient and in most cases, care is immediate. Many ToC patient problems, like pressure ulcers for example, happen within the first 48 hours after surgery.

There are a number of application-related standards in use within the healthcare landscape. The most commonly cited include:

Health Level Seven (HL7): A set of international standards for the transfer of clinical and administrative data between software applications used by various healthcare providers. These standards focus on the application layer, which is layer 7 in the OSI model cited earlier.

Digital Imaging and Communications in Medicine (DICOM): A standard for handling, storing, printing, and transmitting information in medical imaging. It includes a file format definition and a network communications protocol.

Systematic Nomenclature of Medicine (SNOMED) Clinical Terms: A systematically organized collection of medical terms providing codes, synonyms, and definitions used in clinical documentation and reporting. Sometimes referred to as SNOMED CT, many consider it the most comprehensive, multilingual clinical healthcare terminology in the world.

The International Statistical Classification of Diseases and Related Health Problems (ICD): An international standard diagnostic code tool for epidemiology, health management, and clinical purposes.

Health IT Standardization

As noted, regulation of health IT is an important strategy to encourage healthcare administrators to adopt systems that use standardized data elements which are harmonized across vendors and facilities. Adoption and use of standardized data elements across the different types of IT vendors used by different healthcare organizations facilitate continuity of care, improved consistent communication, and the enhanced electronic exchange of personal health information as LTPAC residents move between settings for various reasons. One regulatory action reserved in the IMPACT act encouraged standardized items within quality measure domains related to cognitive status/functional status, skin integrity, medication reconciliation, incidence of falls, and transmission of care preferences (e.g. advanced directives). One outcome of these regulations is improved patient safety.

Technologies for LTPAC Settings

As specialized sites of care, LTPAC provider organizations have unique information, and by extension, software application needs. With the exception of select vendors, most LTPAC application systems are limited to a single care delivery model. Below is a review of the key application needs of the three most common LTPAC provider organizations: nursing homes, assisted living facilities, and home health agencies.

Nursing homes: The applications most common to SNFs partition into the following application categories:

- *Point-of-care*: Applications that allow Certified Nursing Assistants and other users to track residents' care and health, such as their activities of daily living, dehydration risk, skin issues, food intake, weight management, etc.
- *Clinical charting*: Full EMR to document procedures and progress notes, input orders, and send/receive care summaries/transition-of-care documents.
- *Minimum Data Set (MDS)*: The MDS is a tool for implementing standardized assessments and facilitating care management in Medicare or Medicaid-certified nursing facilities. MDS assessments for each resident are electronically tracked and usually integrated with the point-of-care and charting solutions.
- *Medications management*: With the use of assistive technologies like barcode support for the scanning of medications, electronic medication administration records (eMAR) and electronic treatment administration records (eTAR) allow organizations to automatically track medications/other treatments from order to administration. This system may or may not be included as part of a point-of-care or clinical module.

- *Patient scheduling*: Applications used for the scheduling, tracking, and management of resident visits with staff physicians, or to external facilities.
- *Financials/Billing*: Software for managing resident accounts, including collections of monthly or annual resident fees, and sometimes the full accounting and management of residents' finances.
- *Marketing*: Applications to help with the management and tracking of referrals and/or pre-admissions.

Assisted living facilities: While ALFs and independent living facilities (ILFs) share some similarities with SNFs, they typically do not need the full spectrum of clinical functionalities required by more intensive care settings. That said, software programs targeted to ALF and ILF providers tend to offer the same functionalities as those just outlined for SNFs, with the exception of the EMR and MDS systems. ALFs are also more likely to deploy a medications management and point-of-care system, depending upon the needs of their resident population, than an ILF.

Home health agencies (HHA): Software applications for HHAs require many of the same functionalities as those outlined for SNFs (charting, eMAR, notes, orders, etc.). The distinguishing feature of HHA applications is the need for mobile access by HHA workers. Many of these systems are cloud-based, and use either a mobile-optimized web interface or a native mobile application for tablets and smartphones. The functionality they offer, while similar to the SNF software categories, has features and nomenclature specific to home health workflows and reporting requirements:

- *Point-of-care*: An application that assists with the management and tracking of progress notes, health maintenance, and specific HHA mandates such as the Outcome and Assessment Information Set (OASIS), Outcome-Based Quality Improvement (OBQI) reporting, Home Health

Resource Group (HHRG) scoring, completion of HFCA/
CMS Form 485, etc.

■ *Scheduling*: Application that electronically manages
and tracks mobile workers' and patients' appointments.
Some systems also offer an online scheduling portal for
appointment requests, cancellations, etc.

■ *Billing/Accounting*: Software programs that electronically
bill insurance and self-pay patients, offer electronic claim
scrubbing and CMS-1500 completion and submissions,
electronic remittance notice (ERN) posting, multi-payer
support, request for anticipated payment (RAP) submissions, and case mix calculators. Accounting functions
usually include payroll, inventory management, and
budgeting/forecasting.

■ *Marketing*: Software used to manage patient relationships with functions akin to those of customer relationship management (CRM), including wait-list management,
donor management for nonprofit organizations, track
referrals, etc.

Information System Maturity

A distinguishing feature of the U.S. healthcare system is its
emphasis on advanced technology. Technological advances
manifest at the macro level (e.g. adoption of the EHR to
replace paper-based activities) as well as at the local provider
level. Measuring the progressive maturation of healthcare
technological landscapes, from simple to complex systems, is
crucial in order to provide information system stakeholders a
contextual understanding of the system's adoption of technology as well as the sophistication of their IT capabilities.

The original concept of information system maturity devel-
oped from a stage theory proposed by Nolan in 1973 (Nolan,
Managing the Computer Resource: A Stage Hypothesis, 1973).
Nolan's theory posited that elements in a system move through

a pattern of distinct stages over time and that these stages are identifiable. Nolan in his work proposed the following six stages of growth: (Nolan, Managing the Crisis in Data Processing, 1979)

1. *Initiation*: The introduction of information systems into an organization.
2. *Contagion*: The expeditious spreading of IT into various sectors of the organization.
3. *Control*: An effort to bring order to the chaos experienced in the contagion stage through the use of formalized project management and management reporting systems.
4. *Integration*: Occurs as users become more adept at using technology and perceive real value from its use.
5. *Data administration*: The necessitated administration and management of data to allow for development without chaos and expanding IT expenditures.
6. *Maturity*: Constant growth to include increasing data ownership by end users and stability commensurate with the organization's vision and mission (Hollyhead & Robson, 2012).

The concept of IT maturity and maturity stages are current developments in healthcare (Rocha, 2011). Models exist to assess the general healthcare environment, mobile health, electronic medical records, interoperability, telemedicine, and usability. The HIMSS Analytics EMR Adoption Model (EMRAM) is perhaps one of the most recognized maturation models in the health IT world (HIMSS Analytics, n.d.), but is certainly not the only one of its kind.

An LTPAC-focused information system maturity model, developed with support from the Agency for Healthcare Research and Quality (AHRQ), offers a valued IT assessment and roadmap for LTPAC professionals. Leveraging a national Delphi panel of over 30 LTPAC IT experts, activities in LTPAC organizations supported by health IT were identified, then staged according to their sophistication (*Attributes of IT Sophistication*) and area of activity (*Domains* of *Healthcare*) (Table 2.2). LTPAC organizations can then be "scored" according to the presence, use, and integration of IT systems with internal and external stakeholders to yield a maturity stage. The model reflects six stages of IT maturity ranging from "nonexistent" IT systems (stage 0) to "accessibility of electronic data by residents and/or representatives to drive self-management" (stage 6). The model is innovative in that it is the first national assessment of nursing home IT maturity and maturity stages reflecting IT capabilities, the extent of IT use, degree of IT integration, and the relationship between the maturity stage and nursing home resident outcomes (Quality Measures) in LTPAC settings (Figure 2.1).

Summary

The purpose of Chapter 2 was to conclude the discussion surrounding the complex and confusing U.S. healthcare landscape started in Chapter 1. As one part of the healthcare ecosystem, the technological environment has a significant impact on the operations of LTPAC and other types of healthcare providers.

The chapter opened by reviewing the Open Systems Interconnection (OSI) model of communication. The model presents as a useful framework for understanding how the technology infrastructure allows applications to communicate over a network and is referenced several times in the discussion of the two major divisions of the technology environment, the *technology infrastructure* and *applications*.

The technology infrastructure refers to the hardware and network resources of an information system. The IT infrastructure consists of five components: data; routers, switches, and servers; wired and wireless networks; client terminals and devices; and data storage and data integration.

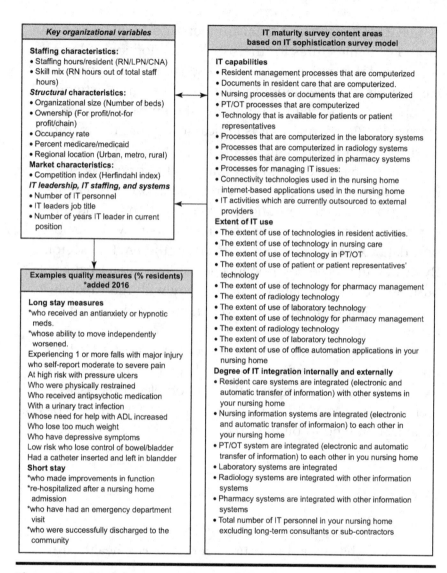

Key organizational variables	IT maturity survey content areas based on IT sophistication survey model
Staffing characteristics: • Staffing hours/resident (RN/LPN/CNA) • Skill mix (RN hours out of total staff hours) ***Structural* characteristics:** • Organizational size (Number of beds) • Ownership (For profit/not-for profit/chain) • Occupancy rate • Percent medicare/medicaid • Regional location (Urban, metro, rural) **Market characteristics:** • Competition index (Herfindahl index) ***IT leadership, IT staffing, and systems*** • Number of IT personnel • IT leaders job title • Number of years IT leader in current position	**IT capabilities** • Resident management processes that are computerized • Documents in resident care that are computerized. • Nursing processes or documents that are computerized • PT/OT processes that are computerized • Technology that is available for patients or patient representatives • Processes that are computerized in the laboratory systems • Processes that are computerized in radiology systems • Processes that are computerized in pharmacy systems • Processes for managing IT issues: • Connectivity technologies used in the nursing home internet-based applications used in the nursing home • IT activities which are currently outsourced to external providers **Extent of IT use** • The extent of use of technologies in resident activities. • The extent of use of technology in nursing care • The extent of use of technology in PT/OT • The extent of use of patient or patient representatives' technology • The extent of use of technology for pharmacy management • The extent of radiology technology • The extent of use of laboratory technology • The extent of use of technology for pharmacy management • The extent of radiology technology • The extent of use of laboratory technology • The extent of use of office automation applications in your nursing home **Degree of IT integration internally and externally** • Resident care systems are integrated (electronic and automatic transfer of information) with other systems in your nursing home • Nursing information systems are integrated (electronic and automatic transfer of informaion) to each other in your nursing home • PT/OT system are integrated (electronic and automatic transfer of information) to each other in you nursing home • Laboratory systems are integrated • Radiology systems are integrated with other information systems • Pharmacy systems are integrated with other information systems • Total number of IT personnel in your nursing home excluding long-term consultants or sub-contractors
Examples quality measures (% residents) *added 2016	
Long stay measures *who received an antianxiety or hypnotic meds. *whose ability to move independently worsened. Experiencing 1 or more falls with major injury who self-report moderate to severe pain At high risk with pressure ulcers Who were physically restrained Who received antipsychotic medication With a urinary tract infection Whose need for help with ADL increased Who lose too much weight Who have depressive symptoms Low risk who lose control of bowel/bladder Had a catheter inserted and left in blandder **Short stay** *who made improvements in function *re-hospitalized after a nursing home admission *who have had an emergency department visit *who were successfully discharged to the community	

Figure 2.1 Model to assess IT maturity.

Applications, the highest level of the OSI model, represent the "face of healthcare IT" to many people. Applications are software programs that "sit" on top of the technology infrastructure or hardware of an information system. Applications in healthcare IT generally fall into one of three areas: administrative applications, financial applications, and clinical applications.

LTPAC IT professionals must understand basic telecommunications architectures for the successful adoption of long-term care information systems. These architectures provide basic levels of understanding for how to design a network to support data exchange between different stakeholders in the system. Furthermore, it is critical to explore the maturity levels of information systems among partners involved in the data exchange to maximize data and information sharing capabilities among people across organizations. Finally, it is important to understand the core functions of the different types of information systems as well as how they support data exchange and care delivery in the PA/LTC sector. By evaluating these components, leaders are able to align business decisions related to technology with the capabilities of the information system to maximize its value for the organization.

Today's LTPAC organizations in general reflect a sophistication in all respects outlined in this chapter. While there still exist sites in the marketplace that rely on electronic assessments like the MDS and OASIS to be their EMR, these types of organization tend to be the exception rather than the rule.

For Discussion

1. Discuss key "health IT capabilities," and how "extent of IT use" has varied in your experience as a healthcare provider.
2. Describe how a greater IT integration may affect patients' safety and access to information.
3. List some assumptions about *IT sophistication* among some of the key organizational variables and expected relationships to quality measures.
4. Explain why it is important to understand different types of telecommunication models as you consider adopting health IT systems.

5. Diagram how a health IT infrastructure might look as you consider the most important capabilities to implement in your facility and their connectivity internally and externally to your facility.

References

Agency for Healthcare Research and Quality (AHRQ). (n.d.). Consumer Health IT Applications. Retrieved from Agency for Healthcare Research and Quality (AHRQ): https://healthit.ahrq.gov/key-topics/consumer-health-it-applications

Alexander, G., L., & Wakefield, D., S. (2009). Information Technology Sophistication in Nursing Homes. *Journal of the American Medical Directors Association*, 10(6), 398–407.

Czaja, S., Sharit, J., Nair, S., & Lee, C. (2008). Older Adults and the Use of E-health Information. *Gerontechnology*, 7(2), 97.

Fisk, A., Rogers, W., Charness, N., Czaja, S., & Sharit, J. (2009). *Designing for Older Adults: Principles and Creative Human Factors Approaches*. Boca Raton, FL: CRC Press.

HIMSS Analytics. (n.d.). EMRAM: A Strategic Roadmap for Effective EMR Adoption and Maturity. Retrieved from HIMSS Analytics: http://www.himssanalytics.org/emram

Hollyhead, A. & Robson, A. (2012). A Little Bit of History Repeating Itself: Nolan's Stages Theory and the Modern IS Auditor. *Information Systems Audit and Control Association Journal*, 5, 46–49.

Ngafeeson, M. (2014). Healthcare Information Systems: Opportunities and Challenges. In *Encyclopedia of Information Science and Technology* (3rd ed.) (pp. 258–267). IGI-Global. Retrieved from Northern Michigan University: https://commons.nmu.edu/facwork_bookchapters/14/

Nolan, R. L. (1973). Managing the Computer Resource: A Stage Hypothesis. *Communications of the ASM*, 399–405.

Nolan, R. L. (1979). Managing the Crisis in Data Processing. *Harvard Business Review*, 115–126.

Rantz, M., L., Galambos, C., Lane, K., Alexander, G., Despins, L., Koopman, R., Skubic, M., Hicks, L., Miller, S., Craver, A., & DeRoche, C. (2017). Randomized Trial of Intelligent Sensor System for Early Illness Alerts in Senior Housing. *Journal of American Medical Directors Association*, 18(10), 86–870.

Rocha, A. (2011). Evolution of Information Systems and Technologies Maturity in Healthcare. *International Journal of Healthcare Information Systems and Informatics*, 28–36.

Welton, J. M., Decker, M., Adam, J., & Zone-Smith, L. (2006). How Far Do Nurses Walk? *MedSurg Nursing*, August, 15(4), 213–216.

Wikipedia. (n.d.). OSI Model. Retrieved from Wikipedia: https://en.wikipedia.org/wiki/OSI_model

Wikipedia. (n.d.). Software Standard. Retrieved from Wikipedia: https://en.wikipedia.org/wiki/Software_standard

SYSTEMS

II

Chapter 3

LTPAC and the Health IT Life Cycle: Decision, Selection, and Acquisition

Learning Objectives

Reading this chapter will help you to

- Outline the four major stages of the systems development life cycle (SDLC) process.
- Identify the types of LTPAC roles that could participate on an SDLC team.
- Explain why analyzing a problem is important to the SDLC Decision stage.
- List the four components of a robust problem statement.
- Identify the types of questions the problem analysis team should address when developing a generalized solution to an identified problem.
- Describe the four steps involved in the Selection phase of the SDLC.

- Detail ways to analyze current business and clinical processes.
- Formulate alternate processes and potential solutions.
- Summarize the factors to consider when making the decision to build or buy a health IT solution.
- Outline the steps organizations progress through when selecting a vendor.

Introduction

As defined in Chapter 1, LTPAC refers to specific types of healthcare provider organizations focused on the provision of care to individuals with some degree of extended care dependency needs. The LTPAC provider market covers a wide range of healthcare services, from care coordination and wellness services for residents living in the community, to skilled nursing services for long-term and short-term nursing home residents. Healthcare leaders in LTPAC provider organizations considering health IT (HIT) solutions to support their care efforts need to devise implementation strategies that not only consider the types of services delivered, but also the people and processes in the healthcare organization.

This chapter and the next look at the array of activities LTPAC HIT leaders should address when pursuing a health IT solution for their organization. Generally referred to as the *systems development life cycle* (SDLC), numerous models exist describing the process for analysis, design, implementation, and operation of an information system. The framework used in this textbook includes the following four stages:

1. Decision
   - Problem Analysis
2. Selection
   - Preliminary Investigation
   - Requirements Analysis

    – Analysis of Alternatives
    – Proposal/Approval
3. Acquisition
    – Building vs. Buying
    – Building
    – Buying
4. Project Management
    – Pre-Implementation
    – Implementation
    – Post-Implementation

The present chapter covers the first three stages, whereas Chapter 4 addresses the Project Management stage.

Decision

The first stage of the SDLC, the Decision, Problem Analysis stage, purposes to clearly define a specific problem the organization faces and then to propose a generalized solution to addressing that concern. By thoroughly analyzing a presenting problem, organizational leaders get a sense as to the extent to which a potential solution involves a health IT solution, if at all.

Before conducting a problem analysis, the first decision the organization must address surrounds the selection of people to be part of the SDLC team. A crucial beginning decision is selecting a qualified project leader who will navigate the entire project and can build and manage high-functioning teams. Though different team members will come and go as the project progresses, it is the project leader's responsibility to choose key project champions throughout different stages of the SDLC. These champions should be affected by the problem being addressed, will most likely use the solution selected, and are intimately knowledgeable of processes of care. In LTPAC settings, teams typically reflect a multidisciplinary approach involving physicians, nurses, nursing assistants, social workers, consultant pharmacists, and rehabilitation and dietary specialists. These clinical disciplines are included because they use health IT system as part of their work, and are integral to the full clinical care a person receives in an LTPAC setting.

Table 3.1 includes a list of potential project champions in the LTPAC setting.

Table 3.1   LTPAC Health IT Project Champions and Leaders

Administrator (Regional or Local)	Environmental Services
Benefits Coordinator	Executive Assistant Managers (Regional or Local)
Business Office Manager	Executive Director/Director (Regional or Local)
Campus Director	Health Information Management
Central Supply	Information Technology Technicians
Chief Executive Officer (CEO)	Medical Records
Chief Financial Officer (CFO)	Minimum Data Set Coordinator
Chief Information Officer (CIO)	Network Administrators
Chief Operations Officer (COO)	Nursing
Chief Nursing Officer (CNO)	Owner
Chief Clinical Officer (CCO)	Quality Management
Chief Medical Officer/Medical Director	Regional Consultant
Clinical Information Systems/ Technology	Scheduling Coordinator
Clinical Services	Senior Vice President
Community Relations	Social Services
Customer Service Representative	Systems Analyst
Education	Transitional Care

Selecting organizational champions and leaders is crucial to signaling to the rest of the organization that from the beginning of the project, everyone will be involved, everyone will use health IT, and that there is no option not to participate (Rizer, Kaufman, Sieck, Hefner, & Scheck McAlearney, 2015). It is most important that all members of the team be involved in the process. The days of the chief executive officer (CEO), chief financial officer (CFO), or chief information officer (CIO) making the decision as to what health IT system to purchase without the input of the team is over. The person or company that controls the capital budget has to be involved. Health IT is usually considered a capital expenditure. This might be the CFO or it could possibly the REIT (a real estate investment trust: a company that owns, and in some cases operates, income producing real estate). There must be buy-in by the team or the chances of acceptance and of successful implementation and use are slim.

Once a team for the problem analysis is in place, they are responsible for addressing the following tasks:

1. Define the Problem
2. Determine the Cause
3. Identify a solution or variety of solutions

Define the Problem

Activities around the decision to adopt health IT can constitute one of the most frustrating stages of the SDLC for some stakeholders involved in the analysis. With IT needs that may seem obvious to some, IT leaders often find certain stakeholders viewing the formality of defining, analyzing, and documenting IT needs a waste of time and resources. Yet Albert Einstein, the great German mathematician, extolled the value of problem definition when he reportedly said, "If I had an hour to solve a problem I'd spend 55 min thinking about the problem and 5 min thinking about solutions" (Einstein, n.d.). While this statement may sound extreme, it suggests that a well-defined problem is key to developing solutions. Although the focus in this section has been on organizational "problems," the concepts discussed also apply to organizational "opportunities." The team should spend time on emerging opportunities for LTPAC provider organizations.

A multiplicity of reasons suggests the investment expended in this phase is warranted. Variances in understanding what health IT can do for patients and the organization, as well as in the value leaders place on different outcomes are too great to leave unaddressed. For example, some leaders place a priority on health IT streamlining clinical workflow, creating a consistent method for clinical staff to track care delivery, and ensuring efficient workflows improve patient safety. Other leaders prioritize health IT as a means to enhance communication between various internal and external stakeholders involved in patient care activities. Some leaders push to acquire a new or updated health IT enterprise system as a way to become a valued partner in the evolving Person-Centric eLongitudinal Spectrum of Care (Derr, 2016). As legislation and regulations continue to push the healthcare system from an episodic fee-for-service model to a value-risk model, it is almost "mandatory" that LTPAC organizations upgrade their clinical technology in order to be preferred providers within their communities. Whatever the reason for health IT adoption, leaders must be certain that the decision aligns with the strategic vision and values of the organization and that the type of IT adopted fits with the expected future.

In defining a problem, teams can develop a clear problem statement by addressing the following four issues.

1. *Core concern*: Describe the problem or issue in terms of the failure encountered.
2. *Occurrence*: Identify when and where the failure is occurring.

3. *Size*: Describe the magnitude of the failure.
4. *Impact*: Describe the impact of the problem on the healthcare organization.

Determine the Cause

Once defined, the problem analysis team is in a position to explore the factors precipitating the failure. Many tools to investigate the cause of a problem exist, including flowcharting the "current state" and stakeholder interviews. One common mistake teams make during this phase is to be too myopic regarding the role of technology as a cause of a system failure. Recognizing that systems involve people, processes, and technology, any one (and in some cases all three) of these factors may be contributing to the identified failure.

Teams in this stage should also be careful to distinguish between the "symptomatic" or presenting cause of a failure and its root cause. While symptomatic and root causes may sometimes be the same thing, they are often different. A root cause requires the problem analysis team to "unearth" problem sources. One popular technique for conducting a root cause analysis, called the *Five Whys*, comes from the analyze phase of Six Sigma, the DMAIC (define, measure, analyze, improve, and control) methodology. The "Five Whys" is an iterative interrogative technique used to explore the cause-and-effect relationships underlying a particular problem. By repeatedly asking the question "Why?" (five is a good rule of thumb), problem analysis teams can peel away the layers of symptoms which can lead to the root cause of a problem.

Identify Solutions

Having defined the problem and its source, the problem analysis team can now proceed to offer a generalized solution or variety of solutions to explore in the Selection stage. The solutions offered by the problem analysis team should address the following five basic questions:

1. *What is the priority for resolving the problem?* The impact on the organization and the importance of the problem as compared to other issues, problems, and initiatives to which the organization must commit resources, influences the solution's priority. The answer to this question should also align with the organization's strategic information systems (SIS) plan, which outlines the organization's overall technology needs, the technical infrastructure and its future priorities. Most SIS plans offer a timeline, typically on the scale of three to five years, for when major initiatives will begin and end. Some plans even include estimated operating and capital budget projections. In the absence of an SIS plan, healthcare organizations tend to implement technological solutions on an ad hoc basis driven by need (or crisis), popular trends, or by the most persuasive stakeholders.

2. *Is the goal to solve the symptom or root cause of the problem?* In a perfect world, the goal should always be to solve the root cause. However, sometimes it may be adequate to address the symptom alone. Referred to as a "workaround," organizations often favor this approach when solving the root cause is too costly, is dependent on unavailable resources, or is for a future initiative.

3. *Will the approach to solving the problem rely on people, process, technology, or some combination of the three?* One of the challenges IT leaders face in this part of the "Decision" stage is the propensity to favor health IT solutions. However, not all solutions require a technology change. Current systems analysis thinking takes a much broader view of the "system" than limiting the solution to technological fixes. Systems analysis recognizes that solutions must consider people, processes, and technology, and how these work together to create value for the

healthcare organization. IT leaders must concede that perhaps technology is not always the answer to a system failure.

4. *What is the broader impact of the solution, and are there any unintended consequences?* An important role of the problem analysis team is to make sure that fixing one problem does not precipitate another failure.

5. *Does the problem reveal a wider opportunity for improvement?* Through the investigation of the problem, the team may uncover a pattern of problems or related needs that requires a more extensive solution. In this case, the originating problem may kick off a preliminary investigation into a broader set of needs that may go beyond the current solution or process to implementing a new solution.

Selection

Having identified a generalized solution or solutions to explore, the next phase of the SDLC is to settle on a recommended solution. The goal of this stage is to develop a specific solution to present to the organization's leaders for approval. The Selection phase consists of four steps towards selecting a health IT solution:

- Preliminary Investigation
- Requirements Analysis
- Analysis of Alternatives
- Proposal/Approval

Preliminary Investigation

The first step in the Selection phase is to determine the organization's need for the generalized solution coming out of the Decision phase of the SDLC. Usually sponsored by the leadership of the organization and conducted by a team of analysts and subject matter experts, the needs assessment purposes to answer three basic questions:

1. What is the need or potential value to the organization of the proposed solution?
2. What is the scope of the solution?
3. Is the solution feasible, given the current technological and operating environment, and if not, what are the major gaps?

The level of effort invested in the preliminary investigation varies by the scope and complexity of the type of solution explored. For large expensive projects, organizations typically supplement the needs assessment with a feasibility study or readiness assessment. Designed to address the organization's ability to implement a solution as well as to identify gaps that need to be filled before undertaking the initiative, these expanded efforts tend to focus on the technological aspects of a proposed solution.

Vendor offerings can be a useful resource for team members during the preliminary investigation as the materials may uncover opportunities that may not have surfaced in the needs assessment. Team members should be cautious in their use though, so as not to bias the results of the needs assessment. The allure of examining new vendor products early in the needs assessment can distract the team from focusing on the organization's real needs. Any review of vendor solutions at this point should be at a high level, involve the examination of a limited set of solutions, and is best reserved for one of the last steps in the needs assessment. A measured, objective approach by the team is critical in this stage given the propensity by some to "jump ahead" and define specific solution requirements and how the solution should be implemented, or to focus on a particular product or vendor solution.

Several possible outcomes can emerge from the preliminary investigation:

1. The findings may justify moving forward with a more detailed assessment of the requirements, cost–benefit analysis, and options.
2. The findings may uncover a broad set of needs, of which only some warrant moving on to the Requirements stage.
3. The findings may determine that the needs do not warrant moving on to the Requirements stage at the current time.

Requirements Analysis

The requirements analysis (aka *business requirements*) section is arguably the most involved and critical stage of the Selection phase. Here the team develops a detailed description of what the proposed solution should do, including defining inputs, outputs, processing, performance, and security. The goal of this stage is to either describe the solution in sufficient detail to support the design and implementation of the solution or to support the selection of a vendor product. The team during this stage must create comprehensive, detailed technical specifications that not only cover the function of the system or applications, but also address nonfunctional issues such as information infrastructure. Once the requirements are set, the team can estimate the solution's cost, resource demands, and implementation schedule with a much greater degree of confidence than during the Needs Assessment stage. Requirements can also play an important role for laying the basis for testing.

Some question the need for defining requirements, especially in LTPAC health IT initiatives, given the limited number of vendor products in the marketplace. The effort applied to defining requirements does not seem worth it when vendor solutions are restricted. Teams should avoid this thinking because the defined requirements can provide an objective basis for selecting among competing vendor solutions. Moreover, the requirements definition can serve as the basis for a request for proposal (RFP) or request for information (RFI) from vendors and may uncover vendor deficiencies that, once known, vendors may elect to address.

The requirements analysis is a significant step in the whole SDLC process, largely because of the risks associated with missing or misinterpreting a requirement. As all of the later steps of the SDLC depend on a solid foundation of requirements, changes to requirements later in the life cycle will require redesign, reconstruction, and retesting, depending on when the team discovers the omission. This in turn increases the cost and elongates the schedule for the initiative. Failure to identify requirements can be particularly onerous when selecting a vendor product as changes to the vendor software are frequently queued within a list of needs from other vendor clients.

Some of the key current- and future-state areas of technical specifications that the team should address include:

1. *System and network architecture*: Does the system have to fit into the organization's existing architectures or may it vary? The information infrastructure must be able to support today's business requirements and anticipate emerging or future business requirements. In general, a healthcare organization should have a process in place to examine or evaluate emerging trends and technologies. It is best to conduct this evaluation on a regular basis as new technologies emerge or as the organization adopts existing technologies.
2. *Security and data encryption*: Does the system integrate into the organization's security standards?
3. *Disaster recovery*: What is the recovery time objective (RTO), or the time it will take to recover the system in a disaster? What is the recovery point objective (RPO), or acceptable restoration timeframe? As the number of

electronic health records increases, business continuity emerges as a key concern for IT leaders. Organizations must plan for various types of disasters, whether natural or manmade. Storing data at an off-site location is a minimal requirement. Many healthcare providers negotiate contracts with disaster recovery vendors to retain not only copies of data but also the capability to restore entire systems. Larger organizations may own multiple data centers in which they may mirror their data. Networks must be in place to access these remote sites. The business continuity plan must not only ensure that the remote sites are in place but must test the plan at frequent intervals to make certain that it can execute.

4. *Data conversion*: What are the data conversion options if converting from one system to another with different data models?

5. *Response times*: What are the expected response times and response time measures?

6. *System backups*: What are the backup options? How long will backups run for?

7. *System monitoring*: How will system monitoring occur? Will it fit into the organization's existing monitoring infrastructure?

8. *Change management*: How does the vendor of a newly purchased system handle changes? Is there a regular schedule? Does the schedule consider customer convenience?

9. *Availability*: What are the availability requirements? What is the downtime associated with system upgrades?

10. *Time zone and daylight savings time support*: Does the system support multiple time zones, especially if the organization has facilities in different time zones? Are system outages required for spring or fall clock changing?

11. *Standards*: Are system integration standards such as HL7, ICD10, or DICOM, supported?

12. *Government regulations*: Does the system meet current government regulations? What is the vendor commitment for turnaround of new regulations?
13. *System integration*: Will the system automatically integrate with the other healthcare systems and medical devices in the enterprise, or will it cost more to integrate it?
14. *Usability*: How accessible is the system for persons with disabilities as well as for users of mobile devices? HIMSS offers a Health Usability Maturity Model, which has five phases: (HIMSS North America, n.d.)
    1. *Unrecognized*: Lack of awareness of usability.
    2. *Preliminary*: Sporadic inclusion of usability.
    3. *Implemented*: Recognized value of usability and small teams using it.
    4. *Integrated*: Utility benchmarks are implemented with a dedicated user experience team.
    5. *Strategic*: Utility well understood, mandated, budgeted, and with results used strategically in the organization.
15. *Workflow definitions*: What are the desired workflows? Business process reengineering (BPR) is the analysis and redesign of workflows in order to optimize end-to-end processes and automate non-value-added tasks. BPR represents a fundamental rethinking of business processes to achieve improvements in performance measures such as cost, quality, service, and speed. Many organizations today employ Lean or Six Sigma to reengineer their processes. Lean focuses on creating more value for customers with fewer resources, whereas Six Sigma strives to eliminate defects in processes on a long-term basis such that output reduces to a level of 3.4 defects per million opportunities (iSixSigma, n.d.).
16. *Data management*: Does the system fit the organization's data management policies and procedures for such functions as backup, recovery, and archiving? Healthcare organizations must address a wide variety of issues related to their data. Data Management International (DAMA)

created a maturity model of data governance involving ten data management functions within an organization (Dataversity, 2011). The organization must define a process for addressing the following data management functions, and the design team must ensure that the system fits into the selected process:

- *Data governance*: Involves planning, supervision, and control over data management and the use of the data.
- *Data architecture management*: An integral part of the enterprise architecture.
- *Data development*: Includes the analysis, design, building, testing, deployment, and maintenance of data.
- *Database operations management*: Provides support for structured physical data assets.
- *Data security management*: Ensures privacy, confidentiality, and appropriate access.
- *Reference and master data management*: Entails the management of golden versions and replicas.
- *Data warehousing and business intelligence management*: Enables access to decision support data for reporting and analysis.
- *Document and content management*: Includes storing, protecting, indexing, and enabling access to data found in unstructured sources, such as electronic files and physical records.
- *Metadata management*: Includes integrating, controlling, and delivering metadata.
- *Data quality management*: Means defining, monitoring, and improving data quality.

17. *Emerging clinical technology*: Health IT is a constantly evolving industry with numerous innovations emerging (e.g. the Cloud for storage and analytics; Telehealth for Monitoring and patient follow-up; Telemedicine for consultation; etc.). It is important for the analysis to keep an eye on disruptive technologies entering into the market.

Partnering with a few vendors is one way to keep abreast of market advances without being beholden to any one vendor's agenda.

A requirements analysis typically progresses through the following four steps:

1. Current-state analysis
2. Future-state analysis
3. Prioritization
4. Stakeholder sign-off

1. *Current-state analysis*: This analysis details how current processes and information solutions work. At a high level, the current-state analysis identifies fundamental business processes the solution will ultimately need to support. At a more detailed level, the current-state analysis describes current process supports, as well as current deficiencies. Current-state analysis is most important when there is an established set of processes and practices that are subject to change with the deployment of a new solution.

   The techniques used for collecting current-state information are similar to those used in the needs assessment. Part of the current-state analysis involves the identification of process and system deficiencies tagged for future interventions, as well as of those identified by regulations and/or standards from internal and external sources. Teams can detect process deficiencies in various ways:
   - By participating in the development of the current-state analysis.
   - From the analysis itself.
   - Through the examination of performance metrics.

   One of the challenges teams face in conducting a current-state analysis is to differentiate between a true requirement, carried forward from the current to the future state, and what is an artifact of the current-state process itself. Because the current state can bias the group, some teams limit the time and effort spent on the current state, focusing more on high-level requirements.

2. *Future-state analysis*: In the future-state analysis, the team views current-state deficiencies through the lens of the initiative's objectives in order to determine the "what" of the solution. One challenge teams encounter in the future-state analysis is remaining focused on the business requirements of the solution and not on determining the "how" of a solution.

3. *Prioritizing*: Once the current and future state requirements of the solution are established, the team must effectively communicate to stakeholders how the solution will bridge the gap between the current state and future state. Teams may use the following resources to help guide their prioritization efforts:
   - Best practices implemented in other organizations.
   - Desired outcomes, not tasks.
   - Focusing on the problem identified in the current state.
   - National and international standards for health IT.

4. *Stakeholder sign-off*: Sign-off on the requirements by key stakeholders is critical. Sign-off is not a simple signature of agreement, but a commitment by leaders to understand and accept the requirements as adequate to deliver the proposed solution's anticipated benefits. The sign-off should not occur until a thorough walk-through of the requirements and related process changes has occurred with the stakeholders. The sign-off should clearly state that the requirements are complete and comprehensive, and that the stakeholders are committed to delivering the benefits of the solution once implemented. Sign-off reduces the chance of confusion over exactly what the requirements are and serves as a baseline for change requests.

Analysis of Alternatives

Once the analysis required to define the solution has occurred, the team needs to consider alternative solutions. While a team's recommended solution may be "rock solid," this is no guarantee leaders will approve the solution. Most healthcare organizations operate tight budgets and the competition for scarce resources can be fierce. Prudent teams prepare for denials by presenting leaders with choices:

1. *Do nothing*: Here the team addresses what would happen if the organization did nothing to address the need. The conversation here points out the costs to the organization of not moving forward.
2. *Enhance the existing system*: This alternative focuses on how much benefit the organization can derive from the existing system.
3. *Partially implement the proposed solution*: This hybrid solution projects the benefits derived from a limited implementation of the proposed solution, or perhaps a phase-in of the full solution over an elongated period.

Proposal/Approval

The final step in the Selection phase is presenting the recommended approach to the stakeholders and decision-makers, as well as obtaining their approval. Teams should look to win enthusiastic support from the approvers in order for the proposed solution to be successful. While unanimous support is not necessary, it is unwise to proceed with a major initiative unless it has broad and overwhelming support from most stakeholders, and no strong, significant resistance. Initiatives that proceed with only tacit approval run enormous risks of failure.

To ensure success in this stage, the team should review a "final draft" of the proposal with stakeholders prior to presenting the proposal to the decision-makers as a final proposal. Ideally, team representatives provide frequent updates to stakeholders on the team's progress and thus will be prepared to support the proposal. While organization executives are ultimately responsible for approving and funding the proposal, endorsements from physicians, nurses, ancillary department staff, operations staff, and others are required. While these stakeholders may not sign off on the proposal, their endorsement and commitment to the solution is nonetheless essential to its implementation.

The executive presentation is where the decision-makers receive the proposal. The proposal's main presenter should be the initiative's business sponsor with backup from the technical group as needed. If it is a clinical project, a clinician should be involved in the presentation. If the initiative has a high price tag, a representative from finance should be present with a cost–benefit analysis and proposed budget. The executive presentation must clearly state what the team is asking the leaders to approve, as well as the cost and resources required to implement the solution. While many of the details of the resourcing and scheduling will be refined as the project plan is developed, executives must make a decision with the best information possible. If the executives endorse the proposal, the team move on to acquiring the solution.

Acquisition

At this stage of the SDLC, the design team should now have the information it needs to acquire the approved solution. The "Build versus Buy" decision, whether to build the system internally or proceed to the creation of an RFP for a buy decision, is a significant one that many companies face when addressing their health IT software needs. If the team is unsure whether a commercial product exists to meet the specifications, the next step should be to produce an RFI.

The following lists a number of factors the design team should consider when making the decision to build or buy:

1. *IT strategy*: What is the overall strategy for clinical and financial technology? Are most systems internally developed or purchased?
2. *Core versus noncore systems*: Is the system key to the success of the organization or ancillary?
3. *Commodity versus competitive advantage*: Is the system a commodity, such as payroll or word processing, or specific to a healthcare line of business, such as a surgery center?
4. *Maturity*: Is the internal IT department mature enough for internal development? Is the market mature enough to have a wide choice?
5. *Requirements fit*: Does the product meet the critical requirements?
6. *Cost and value*: Does a product meet the cost requirements including implementation, support, maintenance, and upgrades? What are the ongoing maintenance costs of internally built solutions, including retaining the knowledge of the developers?
7. *Time and timing*: How long will it take to develop versus acquire? How long will it take to implement? How long will it take to get updates from the vendor versus in-house changes?
8. *Political factors*: Does a particular vendor influence the decision? Does the project sponsor have a bias?
9. *Regulatory support*: What is the record of accomplishment of the vendor in providing regulatory support versus the experience of meeting those requirements in-house?
10. *Platform*: Does the vendor support the organization's preferred platforms, including their hardware, network, security, and infrastructure?
11. *Integration*: How well will the vendor product integrate with other products in the organization's portfolio?

12. *Life cycle cost estimate*: What are the overall costs over five to ten years to deploy, implement, and support the system?

Build

If the decision is to build the system, the membership of the design team should change to reflect technical members, such as data modelers, technical architects, and application developers. Building a system is complex and an activity most LTPAC organizations elect not to pursue. Readers interested in learning more on this subject are encouraged to explore resources beyond the present textbook.

Buy

If the decision is to buy the system, the next step is to create an RFP to find a vendor offering a system that meets the specified requirements. The technical requirements represent the most important parts of the RFP. When presented with unclear requirements, vendors may make their own assumptions and submit vastly different bids than what the organization really wants or needs. Differing assumptions that surface after the signing of a contract may lead to project delays, the inability of the vendor to deliver the product, or litigation. When a contract gets to the point of litigation, unclear requirements make it much harder to plead a case.

There are typically four steps organizations progress through when selecting a vendor:

1. *RFIs and RFPs*: An RFI gathers information about which vendors are able to meet the organization's high-level project requirements. An RFI solicits background information on companies and their capabilities, and typically includes:
   - *An introduction*: This notes that the RFI is for information and planning purposes only.

     – *A background*: Briefly describes relevant factors lead-
      ing to the RFI request.
     – *The requirements*: Describes what responding ven-
      dors must address, including requirements in the
      areas of:
- Project management support
- Reporting
- Development, integration, implementation, maintenance
- Training and education
- Adoption reporting
- User acceptance and field-testing support

     – *Submittal information*: Information about what
      responding vendors need to know in regard to where,
      when, and how to submit the proposal.

An RFP provides the official request for vendors to submit how they will meet the requirements, which are more
defined and include timelines and budget details.

2. *Evaluation activities*: The evaluation process includes:
     – *An evaluation of RFPs*: The team independently
      reviews and scores responses based on the vendor's
      ability to meet the requirements, followed by a team
      discussion and consensus on a final score. This pro-
      cess helps identify which vendors can meet the orga-
      nization's needs and provides the first opportunity to
      eliminate any vendor that cannot.
     – *Comparison to an IT strategic plan*: The team com-
      pares vendor responses to the organizational IT strate-
      gic plan to see how the offered solution aligns to the
      overall plan.
     – *Compliance with regulatory requirements*: The team
      evaluates all vendors against any relevant government,
      regulatory, and/or security requirements.

3. *Due diligence*. Once the team reduces the list of possible
   vendors to a manageable number, the team conducts
   additional research, to include:

- *Background checks*: Background checks include the vendor's financial stability, market share, and customer satisfaction, as well as their time in the market.
- *Demonstrations*: Seeing the solution in action, albeit a generic version of the product, can greatly benefit the team's product evaluation. Whenever possible, the same team members should attend all scheduled demonstrations in order to properly compare and score each option prior to final selection.
- *Site visits*: Visiting a site that has already worked with a vendor and implemented their solution provides an opportunity to work with others in the industry that have faced similar challenges. Site visits can reveal how to customize the vendor's system during the implementation to fit defined workflows and processes. It is optimal if the project team, and not the vendor, chooses what sites to visit, but this is not always an option.
- *Client references*: Contacting the vendor's clients for references offers a suitable alternative to a site visit. While the selection team will not see a live version of the system, the team can ask the same questions as they would during a site visit. Web meeting technologies allow for demonstrations of how a client is using the system without the travel.
- *Road map analysis*: The product roadmap details how a vendor intends to deliver on its promises. Analyzing the roadmap provides valuable insight into the potential challenges vendors might face in delivering on their promises.
- *External research*: External, independent industry research companies like KLAS, offer providers feedback from their peers on the capabilities and performance of specific health IT vendors. KLAS began reporting on LTPAC health IT vendors in 2016.

4. *Making the selection*: Throughout the buying process, the team should be meeting regularly to evaluate and score the remaining vendors against new information obtained from demonstrations, site visits, etc. The team shares its comments and final evaluations of the remaining vendors with the contracting representative, leading to the vendor negotiation process. The contract representative negotiates with the remaining vendors to obtain the best solution for the organization; to include cost, software, hardware, implementation services, support, and maintenance. Contract negotiations are an iterative process typically involving multiple modifications to a legal document. Though each requested modification to the contract adds time to the solution acquisitions timeframe, the selection committee, as well as a legal representative, should carefully review all documents sent to the organization from the vendors because once the organization signs the contract, that is a binding contract.

Based on the negotiations and the final offer from each of the remaining vendors, the team then selects the vendor they will use for the recommended solution. The team should document the justification of the selection in case anyone (vendors included) contests the award. The final agreements often include items such as the payment schedule, vendor and client responsibilities, delivery schedule, penalties for not meeting deadlines, as well as the termination conditions and process.

Summary

Numerous systems development life cycle (SDLC) models exist describing the process for the analysis, design, implementation, and operation of an information system. This textbook uses a four-stage model. This chapter addresses the Decision,

Selection, and Acquisition stages, with the Project Management stage deferred to Chapter 4.

A crucial decision that organizations must address at the start of an SDLC is to get the "right people" on the SDLC team, to include a strong, qualified project leader. SDLC teams in LTPAC provider organizations typically reflect a multidisciplinary approach involving physicians, nurses, nursing assistants, social workers, and rehabilitation and dietary specialists.

SDLC teams in the Decision stage are responsible for defining the problem the organization is facing, determining the cause of the failure as well as identifying a generalized solution to pursue. While some view the formality of defining, analyzing, and documenting IT needs a waste of time and resources, a well-defined problem is key to developing a solution. Understanding why the problem is occurring is another significant step during the Decision stage as a robust analysis recognizes systems fail because they involve people, processes, and technology. With a well-defined understanding of the problem and its cause, SDLC teams are in a position to offer generalized solutions to address a system failure.

The second stage of the SDLC, Selection, purposes to develop a specific solution to present to the organization's leaders for approval. The Selection phase consists of four steps towards selecting a health IT solution: preliminary investigation; requirements analysis; analysis of alternatives; and proposal/approval. The activities involved in the requirements analysis are quite extensive, yet critical to the success of the SDLC process.

The third SDLC stage, Acquisition, occurs once the organization's leaders approve the SDLC team's recommended solution. Organizations in acquiring a solution can elect to "build" or "buy" the desired product. "Build" decisions are quite complex and beyond the scope of this book. Purchase decisions are common outcomes in LTPAC SDLC efforts and frequently require organizations to create RFPs. Contract negotiations are an iterative process requiring the SDLC team and legal counsel to be methodical in their reviews of contract modifications given the binding nature of the agreement once signed.

For Discussion

1. Apply the SDLC model to a specific type of technology that might be useful in your healthcare setting, discuss team members that should be involved in the decision-making process, how selection of the technology should proceed, and who is responsible during the Acquisition phase.
2. Suppose the team decides that usability is an extremely important consideration in the first three phases of the SDLC process. Summarize usability issues you might consider most important and why. Outline a plan to test usability at every stage and acceptable criteria.
3. Appraise how the clinical workflow of various disciplines fits into the evaluation of health IT. Discuss the process and frequency of workflow assessments.

References

Dataversity. (2011, November 29). Assessing Data Management Maturity Using the DAMA DMBOK Framework – Part 1. Retrieved from Dataversity: http://www.dataversity.net/assess-ing-data-management-maturity-using-the-dama-dmbok-frame-work-%E2%80%93-part-1/

Derr, J. F. (2016, August 23). The Value Proposition of Long-Term and Post-Acute-Care Coordination. Retrieved from VBP Monitor: http://www.vbpmonitor.com/news/item/182-the-value-proposition-of-long-term-and-post-acute-care-coordination

Einstein, A. (n.d.). Albert Einstein > Quotes > Quotable Quote. Retrieved from Goodreads: https://www.goodreads.com/quotes/60780-if-i-had-an-hour-to-solve-a-problem-i-d

HIMSS North America. (n.d.). HIMSS Usability Maturity Model Assessment Tool. Retrieved from HIMSS: http://www.himss.org/himss-usability-maturity-model-assessment-tool

iSixSigma. (n.d.). Statistical Six Sigma Definition. Retrieved from iSixSigma: https://www.isixsigma.com/new-to-six-sigma/statistical-six-sigma-definition/

Rizer, M. K., Kaufman, B., Sieck, C. J., Hefner, J. L., & Scheck McAlearney, A. (2015). Top 10 Lessons Learned from Electronic Medical Record Implementation in a Large Academic Medical Center. *Perspectives of Health Information Management*, Summer, 1–9.

Chapter 4

LTPAC and the Health IT Life Cycle: Project Management

Learning Objectives

Reading this chapter will help you to

- Identify the three distinct phases of the SDLC Project Management stage.
- Explain the components involved in the Pre-Implementation phase.
- Differentiate the varied implementation strategies organizations can pursue.
- Discuss the importance of testing during the Pre-Implementation step.
- Identify activities the SDLC team could do before system activation.
- Summarize the SDLC's response to end user suggestions during the go-live period.
- Discuss the importance of reviewing and refining documentation after the system is live.

Introduction

Chapter 3 introduced the *systems development life cycle* (SDLC) framework used in this textbook. This framework consists of four stages: Decision; Selection; Acquisition and Project Management. The first three stages of the framework (Decision; Selection; Acquisition) were covered in Chapter 3 and focused on activities LTPAC provider organizations undertake in acquiring a health IT solution to address a clearly defined problem. Once the organization acquires the solution, they enter into the Project Management (PM) stage, the focus of the present chapter. Arguably the most intensive stage of the SDLC, PM can be broken into three distinctive phases:

1. Pre-Implementation
2. Implementation
3. Post-Implementation

Pre-Implementation

The organization's leaders up to this point, are committing resources (oftentimes a significant amount) on the promise health IT will pay dividends for the organization by addressing the defined problem. It is incumbent the SDLC team employ the recommended solution in the most efficient and effective manner possible. The PM activities the SDLC team carries out before implementing the health IT solution are very significant as they can determine the success or failure of an IT initiative.

The management of the health IT project before the solution "goes live" involves the following steps:

1. Planning
2. Change Management
3. Implementation Strategies

4. Solution Customization
5. System Integration
6. Manuals and Training
7. Activators

Planning

All implementation projects start with a PM plan. Projects fail due to the lack of planning, poor planning, or not following the plan. The PM plan outlines how to accomplish the project. The following are a number of topics the PM plan addresses:

■ Project scope
■ Risk management
■ Change management
■ Training
■ Testing
■ Issue management
■ Work breakdown structure
■ Communication
■ Activation

Once the project sponsor approves the PM plan, the SDLC project leader conducts a kick-off meeting with all stakeholders. Designed to ensure those involved and those impacted have a shared understanding of the project, the kick-off meeting agenda often covers the following items:

■ The project's scope
■ How the project is to be managed
■ How changes are to be requested, analyzed, and approved
■ Potential risks and strategies to mitigate their impact
■ Introduction of the project team and their roles
■ High-level milestones and a schedule
■ The communication plan

Change Management

The solution implemented should require some degree of organizational change. Planning for change is critical for the staff to embrace the implemented solution.

1. *Change Management team*: The SDLC team should establish a Change Management team. This team is responsible for defining a plan for managing change within the organization resulting from the implemented solution. Taking into consideration organizational culture and politics, the plan includes a strategy for breaking down resistance and encouraging staff acceptance. The team should include a senior member of the organization on the team. The presence of an executive on the team signals to the rest of the organization the leader's commitment to the health IT solution. The team should also include members from all affected areas so they have a sense of ownership of and commitment to the project's success.
2. *Adoption*: The adoption of a solution ties closely with users' perceptions of how the health IT solution fits within their workflow and the projected impact on end users. The end users have to be ready for the change, which is why their involvement in workflow redesign is critical.

Implementation Strategies

Another consideration the SDLC team needs to address early in the project surrounds the approach for implementing the health IT solution. There are multiple strategies for implementing a new system. The SDLC needs to determine which one is right for the organization.

1. *Big bang*: An approach where the solution goes live with all functionality, in all locations at the same time. This approach requires a considerable amount of coordination

to ensure all areas are ready, with hardware in place, training completed, and enough support staff available.

2. *Phased*: The phased approach can take one of two forms.
   - *By location*: An approach where the solution goes live with all functionality one location at a time. This strategy extends the duration of the activation activity, but allows insights gained from earlier implementations to pass down to the queued locations.
   - *Functionality*: An approach where the solution goes live in all locations with one functionality at a time. Similar to the phased by location approach, this strategy also extends the duration of the activation and allows users to acclimate to the system before utilizing it fully.

3. *Pilot*: An approach where the solution goes live in one location as a pilot test, and then on to others in the organization as a "phased" or "big-bang" install. This allows the team to learn from a small group before going live with the entire user community.

4. *Like for like*: An approach where the solution goes live with the same functionality that was in place prior to the project. This strategy is used when replacing a legacy system or during an upgrade to decrease the complexity of the activation and decrease the impact on end users.

Solution Customization

Refining the vendor's solution to meet the organization's needs is a very involved step in the Pre-Implementation stage. The vendor should provide training to the project team on how to make changes to their product.

The SDLC team needs to address two key activities during this step.

1. *Change/Version Management*: In customizing the solution, the project team should be cognizant of how to

handle changes during the project. Requests to change the scope of the project or some requirements during the execution phase are bound to occur. Having a defined process for evaluating each request to determine its impact on the project helps prevent "scope creep." The Change Management plan cited earlier should identify who can submit changes, how to evaluate changes, what documentation is required, and who makes the final decision.

2. *Testing*: The primary purpose of information systems testing is to manage risks of developing, producing, operating, and sustaining systems. System testing enables the stakeholders to identify the technical and operational limitations of the system under development so that they can be resolved prior to deployment. Testing activities occur throughout the solution customization phase. The test plan developed during the Planning step describes all the different testing activities of the project. The testing plan developed in the Planning step and employed in this step should address the following topics:
   – Testing methodology
   – Testing levels
   – Testing controls
   – Test reports

Testing methodology: The complexity of today's health IT systems has led many provider organizations to buy solutions from vendors and outsource development to companies that specialize in the vendor's product. As a result, the IT staff in many provider organizations have a limited understanding of their system's development history. A well-defined testing methodology is therefore critical to ensure the solution meets the specific needs of the organization. Testing scenarios vary widely among healthcare organizations. That said, testing and standards professionals are in general agreement that a sound testing methodology includes the following steps:

1. Define the test strategy
2. Develop test tools
3. Execute the tests
4. Employ test controls
5. Report test results
6. Conduct a final evaluation

1. *Define the test strategy*: The test strategy is a formal description of how to test a system and addresses all levels of the testing process. The test team analyzes the requirements, writes the test strategy, and reviews the plan with the project team and various end users and stakeholders. The test plan may include test cases, conditions, the test environment, pass/fail criteria, and risk assessment. It will also define the testing scope and objectives, current business issues to consider during the test, testing roles and responsibilities, status reporting methods, test execution methods, industry standards to follow, test automation and tools, measurements and metrics, risks and mitigation, defect reporting and tracking, and change/configuration management.
2. *Develop test tools*: Testing tools are widely available in the commercial market and the specific tool employed will depend on the testing methods. Testing tools involve manual and automated processes.
   - *Manual testing* is simply direct human interaction with a system, testing for apparent defects. A member of the test team plays the role of an end user and tests most features of the application to ensure correct behavior. To ensure completeness of testing, the test team often follows a written test plan that leads them through a set of important test cases. Manual testing is a laborious and time-consuming process and not the most effective in finding certain classes of defects.
   - *Automated testing* uses special software separate from the software under scrutiny. It controls the execution

of tests, compares actual outcomes to predicted outcomes, sets up test preconditions, and performs other test-control and test-reporting functions. One of the most significant benefits of test automation is the ability to duplicate the testing process.

3. *Execute the test*: To execute a test, testing teams generally select one of three approaches: *white-box testing, black-box testing, or* a hybrid of these two called *gray-box testing*. These approaches reflect the point of view a test engineer assumes when executing test cases.
   - *White-box testing* is a method that tests the internal structures or workings of a system. The focus is on how the system is supposed to operate and not on its functionality.
   - *Black-box testing* is a method that tests the functionality of a system. The tester's focus is only on what the system is supposed to do and not on the internal operations of the system.
   - *Gray-box testing* is a testing method that combines the white-box and black-box testing approaches. Here the tester has some knowledge of internal structures but also understands the expected functionalities. Gray-box testing is most useful when performing tests on system upgrades, patches, or modifications.

   Testing levels: The classification of a test execution depends on the *level of development* or the *test objective*. There are three *development-level* tests:
   - *Unit testing*: Performed by checking individual units of source code and sets of one or more computer program modules together with associated control data, usage procedures, and operating procedures to determine if they are fit for use. Intuitively, one can view a unit as the smallest testable part of an application. Unit tests are created by programmers and white-box testers during the development process.

- *Integration testing*: Involves combining individual software modules, or units, and then testing them as a group. Integration testing can be done using any of the box methods, white, black or gray, but is best suited for gray-box testing, where the tester has some knowledge of the internal code of the individual units as well as of the expected system functionality.
- *System testing*: System testing combines all of the integrated components that have successfully passed integration testing and tests them as a single system.

There are four *test objectives*:

- *Stress testing*: Stress testing is a form of testing that determines the stability of a given system beyond its normal operational capacity, often to a breaking point, in order to observe the results. A stress test helps identify vulnerabilities so that a system does not crash in certain conditions (e.g. its available computational resources, denial of service attacks, etc.).
- *Acceptance testing*: Acceptance testing validates that the delivered system meets the user's business requirements.
- *Regression testing*: Regression testing is any type of system testing that seeks to uncover new bugs or errors in an existing functional system exposed to patches, enhancements, or configuration changes. The intent of regression testing is to ensure that a change in software or hardware does not introduce new faults into a system.
- *Operational testing*: Operational testing occurs sometime after deployment (e.g. 90–180 days), and ensures the system is properly used and functioning as intended.

Testing controls: System controls protect the confidentiality, integrity, and the overall management of a system during design, development, testing, and deployment.

Some of the most common types of test controls include:

- *Version control*: As teams design, develop, and test software, it is common for multiple versions of the same software to be running in different sites and for the software's developers to be working simultaneously on updates. Bugs or features of the software present in certain versions may not be in other versions. For the purposes of locating and fixing bugs, it is vitally important to be able to track and regulate source code changes.
- *Security audit*: Security audits are security-vulnerability assessments of a system or application.
- *Change control*: Change control is a formal process for ensuring changes to a product or system occur in a controlled and coordinated manner. It reduces the possibility that unnecessary changes happen to a system without forethought, introducing faults or undoing changes made by other users.

Test reports: Test reporting occurs throughout the testing process and is not reserved for the conclusion of a test event. Stakeholders and sponsors usually expect regular updates on testing activities. A common challenge in reporting tests involves tailoring the reports to the various audiences, clarifying the intent of the testing, explaining how testing is actually done, and understanding which testing metrics are meaningful and why. At the very least, test reports should address the purpose of the test, the systems covered, the organizational risk of deploying the system, testing techniques, the test environment, the most current testing status, and obstacles to testing.

The most important deliverable in a testing project is the final evaluation report. The final evaluation contains the findings, conclusions, and recommendations of the system test. If the system tests successfully, the final evaluation should confirm that the system is able to achieve the expected outcomes and should specifically connect how conducting the test is associated with the stakeholders' return on investment (ROI) expectations. In addition to discussing ROI, the final evaluation report should address common stakeholder questions:

- Does the system meet the organization's quality and performance expectations?
- Is the system ready for users?
- What happens when X people simultaneously use the system?

What are the risks of going live with the system now?

System Integration

It is rare in healthcare today to have a stand-alone IT system. The vast majority of systems share data with another system to some extent. This integration of systems allows data to be shared in multiple systems without manually re-entering data. There are different ways to integrate systems:

1. *Real-time data integration*: This involves the sharing of data upon entry or modification. The standard for this type of integration is Health Level 7 (HL7), which defines the interface message so that what leaves the source system is acceptable to the destination system.
2. *Scheduled data integration*: This is the sharing of data in batches according to a predetermined timeframe (e.g. nightly). The data feed can be accomplished through formatted files or through HL7 messages.
3. *Integration of data from devices*: This involves the feeding of data from a specific device into an application. This type of interface helps decrease manual data entry but may require data verification before being officially accepted within the system.

Regardless of the type of interface, all integration efforts utilize an *interface engine*. An integration engine receives information from the source system and either passes it directly to the destination system or makes some modification to the data before passing it along. Different systems have different requirements for how the data is structured and where in the interface message they expect the specific data to be located.

User and Operational Manuals and Training

As the project nears the go-live stage, it is necessary to educate end users for them to be successful in their use of the system. Training documents are critical for trainer and trainee at this stage. If "hands-on" training is required, a training environment should be set up early in the project to allow the training team to develop materials and use cases practice exercises.

Training classes are tricky to schedule because they need to take place on the system that will ultimately be in use. As a result, the training environment cannot be fully set up until the system's configuration is complete. Training should occur as close to system activation as possible to support user retention of the materials reviewed. Training teams should be prepared to provide "just-in-time" training for those end users unable to make a training class or to remember how to do something. End-user manuals and quick reference guides along with the presence of support staff during the initial week or so will help address "last-minute" trainees.

Activation

Planning for the system going live begins with the selected implementation strategy discussed earlier in this chapter, and continues through the remainder of the project. The organization should work with the vendor to identify activation activities to complete in advance of and those to occur on the go-live day. The actual activities will depend on the specific project. If the organization is moving from a manual process to an automated one or is implementing a new system, the activation could be as simple as having users start using the system. When migrating from a legacy system or upgrading an existing system, the activation activities are more complex and include a period of time when the system is down, or unavailable. A detailed checklist of tasks that occur before and during the activation helps ensure the team does not miss or forget a significant activity. A go-live "dress rehearsal" offers an opportunity to test the process and fix any mistakes that occur, as well as to consider day-of logistics (e.g. where team members will be stationed; if food and drink will be available; what forms of communication will be available for anyone not in the command center; etc.).

Implementation

The Implementation stage reflects the activation of the system. By this time, the organization should be primed and ready for the launch of the health IT solution. The primary function of the team at this point is to support the successful launch of the system. The type and duration of support offered at this stage depends on the impact of the change and the amount of just-in-time training delivered.

Immediately, users will most likely offer suggestions for changing the system. Having a clear process for submitting requests for change will help users know their input is welcome and valuable. That said, SDLC teams should commit to considering the suggestions but not to their implementation. Suggestions frequently arise because the system, workflows, or processes are new and different from the ways users have always done things. Unless suggestions are critical to patient care, teams should document them and review them in about a month to see if those needs still exist.

Post-Implementation

The final step in the PM stage surrounds SDLC team activities once the intensive Implementation support activities have ended. The Post-Implementation stage involves two major focus areas:

1. Managing normal health information systems (HIS) operations
2. Managing disrupted health information systems (HIS) operations

Managing Normal Healthcare Information Systems (HIS) Operations

Once the system is live, the SDLC team moves into an operations and maintenance supportive mode. In light of a live system, the SDLC team should review and refine (if necessary) the following issues in the operations and maintenance documents:

1. *Communication plan*: How end users communicate with the IT department about the new system
2. *Configuration management*: How system configuration changes occur and the levels of approval and documentation required.
3. *Service desk*: How the service desk knowledge base explains the identification and resolution of issues when users contact the service desk.
4. *Data flow*: How data flows from one system to another or from one location in the system to another, along with the dependencies between systems.
5. *Workflow*: How the system fits into users' daily activities.
6. *Downtime procedures*: How end users are to respond when the system is unavailable and how the technical staff will identify and resolve an issue causing downtime.

The management of normal HIS operations often requires SDLC teams to pay special attention to the following operational issues during this stage:

1. *Customer support:* LTPAC provider organizations often provide an IT help desk (or at least a single phone number that goes to an individual who can listen and help end users resolve IT issues) to support customers in their use of the IT system. Organizations should arm their IT support staff with a good knowledge base that allows them to ask the right questions and provide enough information to resolve the issue during the user's first call. When the service desk personnel cannot resolve an issue, the support staff should have a process for providing second-tier support. This often occurs through a ticket management system. Timely feedback and regular updates for the customer are important until the problem is resolved.

2. *Spotting problems and trends:* Throughout the life cycle of any application, it is good practice to look for trends in usage, as well as problems. More specifically, SDLC teams should be looking for trends in levels of system adoption, as well as trends in system performance. Understanding these patterns will help the team in their system performance improvement efforts. Certainly within the first year after an application goes live, analysis should occur to see if the system has actually met the needs identified prior to the system's purchase. This as an evaluation helps the organization realize its expected return on investment.

Managing Disrupted Health Information Systems (HIS) Operations

The other "side of the coin" in managing normal HIS operations involves the management of system disruptions. The criticality of the system within the organization will define the types of planning an organization needs. The following are three plans the SDLC team should review and refine Post-Implementation:

1. The *business continuity plan*: This defines how an organization prepares for and maintains the business functions related to the defined system. This includes the operations and maintenance of the system to ensure stability, the process of resolving issues that could or do cause the system to be unavailable, how the business will continue without the system, and how to recover from an actual disaster. The business continuity plan includes a disaster recovery plan and a downtime plan.

2. *Disaster recovery plan*: The disaster recovery plan focuses on the technical aspects (e.g. data backup and recovery) of recovery after the system goes down. Backups of the data are copied and stored off-site for a predetermined amount of time. For critical systems, some organizations have off-site facilities where they can recover the system from backup tapes if needed.

3. *Downtime plan*: The downtime plan focuses on how to continue to operate without the electronic system. It includes procedures for communication, hard-copy forms for documentation, and plans for data entry once the system becomes available again.

Summary

This chapter focuses on the fourth stage of the SDLC; Project Management (PM). The fourth stage occurs once the organization acquires a health IT solution. The PM stage can be broken into three distinct phases: Pre-Implementation; Implementation, and Post-Implementation. There are a myriad of activities for the SDLC to consider during the Pre-Implementation phase.

Refining the chosen vendor's solution to meet the organization's needs is a very involved step in this stage. Testing to ensure that the system modifications and refinements work is a critical exercise during this stage.

By the time the health IT solution launches, the organization should be well primed and ready. The SDLC team's primary function at this point is to support the system's launch.

Once the intensive Implementation support activities have ended, the SDLC team is in a position to review and refine documents supporting the normal and disrupted management of health information systems (HIS) operations. These reviews involve the organization's customer support activities as well as the business continuity plan.

The complexity of the technologies involved underscores the importance of working alongside one's vendor if purchasing a health IT solution. This partnership is especially true when implementing an enterprise system. If working with multiple vendors, IT leaders need to ensure the vendors "talk" to one another.

For Discussion

1. List some disadvantages and advantages of project management activities during the SDLC life cycle.
2. Provide an overview of the basic steps required for project management activities during the SDLC life cycle.
3. Why is it important to make smart time estimates from the beginning of project management activities?
4. Describe the skills of a project management leader.
5. Break down a process for ensuring that project management activities are meeting the organizational mission.
6. How does a thorough project management plan add value to an organization?

Chapter 5

Privacy and Security in LTPAC Settings

Learning Objectives

Reading this chapter will help you

- Identify the three components of the CIA triad.
- Describe the three approaches to user access controls.
- Describe the components that should be included in an organization's disaster recovery and business continuity plan.

Introduction

Concerns about the privacy and security of health records are not new. Patients have long expected access to their medical records to be restricted and their contents protected, even in the days of paper records. Privacy and security concerns have intensified as healthcare providers have adopted electronic health record (EHR) technologies, which have arguably increased the vulnerability of the data and the magnitude of the potential records one could steal at any one time. Data security fears for many became real in 2015 when the insurance giant Anthem disclosed they had experienced the biggest data breach to date of a healthcare company (Riley, 2015). This admission was a significant healthcare industry moment as it highlighted the interest "bad actors" have in patient data, the vulnerability of the data, and the potential magnitude of these breaches.

LTPAC provider organizations should not passively think their organization's data is of little interest to bad actors. Examples, unfortunately, exist proving otherwise (Oliva, 2014). Many experts argue that healthcare data can be much more attractive to bad actors than financial data (Fox Business, 2014). Indeed, medical identity theft is hard to detect, allowing criminals years to exploit stolen credentials. On the other hand, banks quickly freeze or cancel accounts upon detecting financial data fraud. In today's world, with absent organizational understanding and the adoption of appropriate privacy policies and security safeguards, the threat of compromising events are all too real. LTPAC provider organizations are stewards of sensitive data, and must therefore protect their systems against potential loss and cyberattacks.

The CIA Triad

When considering the most crucial components of data security, healthcare IT security leaders focus on the *confidentiality*, *integrity*, and *availability* of the data. Often referred to as the *CIA triad*, this model provides a baseline standard for evaluating and implementing information security regardless of the underlying system and/or organization (Techopedia, n.d.).

Confidentiality

Confidentiality involves a set of rules or a promise of limiting access or placing restrictions on certain types of information (TechTarget, n.d.a). For LTPAC providers, this means limiting the disclosure of a patient's personal information to comply with policies and regulations, as well as to maintain the trust patients have placed in the facility.

Integrity

Data integrity is the assurance that digital information is uncorrupted and is only accessible or modifiable by those authorized to do so (TechTarget, n.d.c). Integrity involves maintaining the consistency, accuracy, and trustworthiness of data over its entire life cycle. To preserve the integrity of health information, LTPAC leaders need to implement policies and procedures to protect the data from unauthorized modification, deletion, or destruction and to keep it consistent with its source, as well as routinely audit their data management activities.

Availability

Availability in its simplest form is the guarantee of reliable access to information by authorized people (TechTarget, n.d.b). The guarantee includes the protection of information from unplanned destruction, whether by accident, vandalism, or natural disasters, as well as from facility closures/mergers.

Grounded in a basic understanding of the scope and importance of the CIA triad, the remainder of this chapter will review the tools health IT professionals have available to ensure the privacy and security of the information managed in and by their facility. The topics considered are as follows:

1. Data Governance
2. Data Management Controls
3. Risk
4. Disaster Recovery and Business Continuity Planning

Data Governance

Two primary roles in an organization have governance over data privacy and security. One is an expert who understands which privacy laws apply to an organization and how they should be properly interpreted (*senior IT security leader*). This security expert plays a crucial role in most healthcare organizations. The other is a person or persons responsible for the development of and compliance with security policies and procedures (*compliance or risk management leader*).

1. *Senior IT security leader*: Laws in many localities require healthcare organizations to appoint an individual, sometimes with the title of chief information security officer (CISO), to guide how privacy laws apply to the organization. These individuals usually have the following tasks:
   - Assessing and maintaining knowledge of rules and regulations
   - Developing policies and procedures
   - Cultivating organizational and cultural awareness and developing educational plans in support of policies
   - Managing appropriate access for external business partners and ensuring documentation exists in support of such access
   - Monitoring compliance with policies
   - Responding to complaints and other issues that arise
   - Conducting or directing others to conduct scheduled and random access audits
   - Investigating known security breaches and reporting information to appropriate regulatory and/or governmental agencies as required by law
2. *Compliance or risk management leader*: As with privacy rules, it is important for an organization to identify a person or persons who will be responsible for the development of and compliance with security policies and procedures. In many healthcare organizations,

the compliance or risk management leader serves this function.

Based on an understanding of numerous privacy laws and security regulations, both of these leaders develop data governance policies and procedures in support of organizational aims. Together, these policies and procedures reflect the organization's documented rules and processes that its employees and business partners are to follow. As healthcare providers embrace the use of technologies such as EHRs, personal health records, health information exchanges, and e-prescribing, there is a growing body of laws and regulations LTPAC providers need to understand surrounding how organizations may use or disclose health information. One of the laws LTPAC providers should know was contained in the Medicare and Medicaid EHR Incentive Program (also known as the "Meaningful Use" program) (The Office of the National Coordinator for Health Information Technology, 2015). Though LTPAC providers did not participate in the Meaningful Use program, LTPAC organizations are covered entities under HIPAA and the expansion of HIPAA under the HITECH Act. The privacy rule portion of the HIPAA regulation mandates all covered entities appoint a privacy officer to enforce HIPAA compliance by the organization's officers and employees. In some cases, an individual organization may elect to put in place policies that further restrict access for a variety of reasons. For example, the presence in an individual's DNA of a certain genetic marker may not indicate anything today, but as science develops, that same marker could predict a condition that might have negative consequences for the person.

Data Management Controls

To maintain data confidentiality, integrity, and availability, LTPAC providers must put a number of safeguards in place to control access to systems and data. These safeguards fall into three categories:

1. *Administrative*: Administrative safeguards are administrative actions, policies, and procedures that an organization deploys in support of its security aims. Administrative safeguards include such actions as the ongoing education of employees on security requirements and scenarios in which data may or may not be used or disclosed, and developing policies and procedures that provide safeguards within the physical and technical realms.

2. *Technical*: Technical safeguards are electronic means of ensuring that data is not accessible or subject to modifications by a third party. Examples of technical safeguards would include the use of network firewalls, security protocols on any public networks carrying patient data, and the encryption of storage media on laptop computers and mobile devices.

3. *Physical*: Physical safeguards consist of physical measures, policies, and procedures that protect electronic information systems from natural and environmental hazards and unauthorized intrusion. Examples would include data centers that are located outside a flood plain and have redundant sources of power.

Data Management and User Access Controls

One of the most significant roles of the data safeguards surrounds *user access controls*. Understood as the selective restriction of access to a place or other resource, user access controls prevent unauthorized users from having any type of impact on the integrity or availability of health information (Wikipedia, n.d.). The discussion of user access controls can generally be broken down into three categories, sometimes termed the *triple-A approach* (Dyke, Kirby, Shabani, Kato, & Knoppers, 2016):

1. *Authentication*: Authentication is the process of verifying that users are who they say they are before allowing them access to health information. User authentication refers to the human-to-machine transfer of credentials required for confirmation of a user's authenticity, whereas machine authentication involves automated processes that do not require user input (TechTarget, n.d.d). The authentication of active users typically involves one or more of the following:
   - Something the user knows (e.g. a pin or password)
   - Something the user has (e.g. a smart card or token)
   - Something the user is (e.g. a fingerprint or retina scan)
2. *Authorization*: Once a user receives authorization, overseers assign an appropriate "level of access." Data access privileges are ideally set to allow the minimum access necessary in order to perform a job. A user's role within the organization often defines their access. Physicians for example, generally have the ability to place orders, as well as create and sign documents to which a nurse may not have access.
3. *Attestation*: An essential component of an organization's security plan is the ability to audit access to protected data. Attestation (or "Accounting") reports enable an organization to identify any breaches or other policy violations (e.g. looking up coworkers or neighbors in the system). Organizations generate these reports on both a scheduled and random basis.

Risk

Risk involves exposure to some type of danger. In the context of information technology, risks tend to involve scenarios that could have a negative impact on data security or privacy. These risks come from three types of sources:

■ *Humans*: Malicious hackers and employee saboteurs.
■ *Natural disasters*: Floods and tornadoes.
■ *Environmental events*: Power grid failures or chemical accidents.

Once an LTPAC provider organization has developed an awareness of its exposure to risks, the facility leaders should undertake an assessment of the organization's readiness to deal with those threats. These assessments should focus on identifying the gaps that exist between what is required and what actually exists within the organization's operations. The information resulting from a risk assessment should serve to give the organization a realistic assessment of its risks and to identify its vulnerabilities.

The analysis resulting from a risk assessment helps identify the most significant vulnerabilities an organization faces. From there, LTPAC leaders can pursue one of two approaches to reduce the risk to an acceptable level:

1. *Take no action*: Here the current risk level is acceptable to the organization.
2. *Mitigate*: Implement safeguards to reduce risks to an acceptable level.

Disaster Recovery and Business Continuity Plan

In the event of a disaster, facility leaders need to have a plan of how they can recover from the disaster and keep the "business" running. While not entirely the IT staff's responsibility, IT professionals must be involved in the development of these facility *disaster recovery and business continuity plans*. The importance of involving IT personnel in these plans is evident in a 2017 memo to nursing home state survey agencies from the CMS director of the Center for Clinical Standards and Quality/Survey & Certification Group. In this memo, the director explicitly encourages providers to consider cybersecurity as "an element in the development of their emergency plans, risk assessments, and annual training exercises" (Center for Clinical Standards and Quality/Survey & Certification Group, 2017).

Contingency plans include several IT-related elements.

1. *Analysis*: Prioritize applications and data in order of importance to the organization so that a logical sequence of data recovery can occur.
2. *Data backup plan*: Develop detailed plans to ensure the existence of a retrievable backup copy of the organization's critical data.
3. *Disaster recovery procedures*: Plans defining how to restore data after any loss, for any reason, must be documented and accessible to staff.
4. *Emergency-mode operation plan*: Outline downtime plans enabling the organization to continue to operate in emergency mode while access to electronic data is not possible.
5. *Testing*: All contingency plans must be routinely tested and revised to fill gaps that the organization uncovers and to address changing organizational needs and infrastructure.

Summary

Patients, residents, and family caregivers expect their personal health data to remain private and secure with those entrusted with access to the information. As an increasing number of LTPAC provider organizations use information technologies to manage patient data, the challenge of ensuring data privacy and security grows exponentially harder. Yet, for many healthcare providers (and not just LTPAC organizations), privacy and security is an afterthought. LTPAC providers do not have the luxury of ignoring data privacy and security concerns. Nowadays, the question is not "if" but "when" will the data in one's facility be attacked.

Privacy and security is an area where IT leaders do not have the luxury of "on-the-job training." Negligence is fraught with large financial implications and penalties. IT leaders are encouraged to collaborate with their health IT vendors, as well as with vendors specializing in security, privacy, and the HIPAA in LTPAC environments.

For Discussion

1. Having a sound *security plan* in place to collect only what you need, keep it safe, and dispose of it securely can help you meet your legal obligations to protect that sensitive data. Describe the components of a sound security plan.
2. Distinguish differences between the privacy and security of health information.
3. Produce some rules that might be useful in data governance activities that support a strong security plan.
4. How would you evaluate the effectiveness of a security plan?

References

Center for Clinical Standards and Quality/Survey & Certification Group. (2017, January 13). Recommendations to Providers Regarding Cyber Security. Retrieved from CMS.gov: https://www.cms.gov/Medicare/Provider-Enrollment-and-Certification/SurveyCertificationGenInfo/Downloads/Survey-and-Cert-Letter-17-17.pdf

Dyke, S. O., Kirby, E., Shabani, M., Kato, K., & Knoppers, B. M. (2016). Registered Access: A "Triple-A" Approach. *European Journal of Human Genetics*, December, 24(12), 1676–1680.

Fox Business. (2014, September 24). Hackers Want Your Medical Information. Retrieved from Fox Business: http://www.foxbusiness.com/features/2014/09/24/ hackers-want-medical-info-not-credit-card-data. html?utm_source=feedburner&utm_medium=feed&utm_ campaign=Feed:%2520foxbusiness/latest%2520(Internal%2520-%2520Latest%2520News%2520-%2520Text)

Oliva, J. (2014, March 6). Data Breach Hits Assisted Living Concepts, Prompts Damage Control. Retrieved from Senior Housing News: https://seniorhousingnews.com/2014/03/06/ data-breach-hits-senior-living-provider-assisted-living-concepts/

Riley, C. (2015, February 6). Insurance Giant Anthem Hit by Massive Data Breach. Retrieved from CNN Tech: http://money.cnn. com/2015/02/04/technology/anthem-insurance-hack-data-security/index.html

Techopedia. (n.d.). CIA Triad of Information Security. Retrieved from Techopedia: https://www.techopedia.com/definition/25830/ cia-triad-of-information-security

TechTarget. (n.d.a). Confidentiality. Retrieved from TechTarget: http://whatis.techtarget.com/definition/confidentiality

TechTarget. (n.d.b). *Confidentiality, Integrity, and Availability (CIA Triad)*. Retrieved from TechTarget: http://whatis.techtarget.com/ definition/Confidentiality-integrity-and-availability-CIA

TechTarget. (n.d.c). Data Integrity. Retrieved from TechTarget: http:// searchdatacenter.techtarget.com/definition/integrity

TechTarget. (n.d.d). User Authentication. Retrieved from TechTarget: http://searchsecurity.techtarget.com/definition/ user-authentication

The Office of the National Coordinator for Health Information Technology. (2015). *Guide to Privacy and Security of Electronic Health Information.*

Wikipedia. (n.d.). Access Control. Retrieved from Wikipedia: https:// en.wikipedia.org/wiki/Access_control

ADMINISTRATION

Chapter 6

Management and Leadership

Learning Objectives

Reading this chapter will help you

- Understand the series of skills needed to guide and facilitate the development of information technology organizations.
- Effectively communicate in both written and oral presentations to other leaders and the organization, as well as effectively organize complex meeting structures.
- Assess the current systems status by personally interacting with the user community, understanding their perceptions of system and departmental effectiveness, and effectively monitoring performance indicators.
- Develop strategic analyses to better align the IT organization with the organization's mission, vision, goals, and strategies while effectively managing conflicting interests and priorities through effective conflict resolution techniques.
- Learn to balance the necessary relationships with vendors while effectively maintaining a sound business ethic.

- Define roles, responsibilities, and job descriptions for IT-related functions.
- Assure staff competency in information and management systems skills.
- Manage projects and portfolios of projects (e.g. initiate, plan, execute, control, close)
- Manage relationships with vendors (e.g. contract cost, schedule, support, maintenance, performance).
- Facilitate steering committee meetings and/or topics.
- Assure adherence to industry best practices (e.g. change control, project management).
- Maintain system, operational, and department documentation.
- Provide customer service (e.g. service-level management, request tracking, problem resolution).
- Manage budget and financial risks.
- Manage customer relationships with business unit leaders.

Introduction

Healthcare is a complex, dynamic industry. To survive, provider organizations need strong effective leaders and managers. The demand is particularly true for clinical IT professionals in LTPAC provider organizations. Due to limited funds and resources, as well as the corporate structure, LTPAC facilities often lack on-site IT support services. Lack of on-site support increases user frustration and disrupts workflow processes, hampering the effectiveness of the EHRs. Faced with a myriad of unique operational and organizational challenges, individuals occupying these roles need to be highly proficient in leading and managing their organizations.

Before going any further, it is important to recognize that "leadership" and "management" are not synonymous terms. While related, the words do have remarkably different meanings. John P. Kotter, one of the most renowned voices on business leadership and change, defined these differences in the following way (Kotter, 2013):

- *Management* involves planning and budgeting. *Leadership* involves setting a direction.
- *Management* involves organizing and staffing. *Leadership* involves aligning people.
- *Management* provides control and solves problems. *Leadership* provides motivation and inspiration.

Stated differently, if an LTPAC provider organization is like a car, then *leadership* sets the car's overall *direction* whereas *management* focuses on the *drive*. Clearly, both are essential in the delivery of high-quality care. This chapter considers the leadership and management of health IT efforts in LTPAC settings. The review will address the fundamentals of leadership first before addressing the role of today's IT manager.

Leadership

Business leadership is a popular topic in the academic and popular press. As this chapter can only offer a cursory handling of this subject, it may suffice to focus on arguably the two most significant organizational functions of a leader:

1. Setting a *Strategy*
2. Championing *Culture*

Setting a Strategy

Strategy refers to a "plan of action designed to achieve a long-term or overall aim" (English Oxford Living Dictionaries, n.d.). Health IT leaders are responsible for setting the organization's IT direction and approving action plans designed to realize specific goals. Leaders are encouraged to outline and explain their strategic direction to employees through a formalized IT strategic plan. An effective strategic plan includes brief statements reflecting the leader's description of the organization's mission, values, vision, and goals.

1. *Mission*: The *mission statement* explains why an organization exists. All employees of the company should be able to tie the work they do to the company's mission. Once defined, a mission statement should not change unless the business itself changes.
2. *Values*: The *value statement* reflects the principles the company supports and appreciates the most. Most often presented as a list, employees can compare these values against their own personal values to determine whether the values align or conflict with their personal values and/or work assignments.
3. *Vision*: A *vision statement* describes the desired future for the organization. Depending on how far into the future the vision reaches, a vision statement may change with more regularity than the mission statement.
4. *Goals*: *Goals* are specific milestones organizations set out to achieve as they pursue their organizational vision. Clearly articulated goals shaped by the organization's mission and vision serve as guides against which to measure the organization's work. The acronym SMART helps outline the components to include in the development of goals: specific, measurable, attainable, relevant, and time-bound.

Formalized IT strategic plans demonstrating how IT aligns with the strategic goals and objectives of the organization can help employees understand how their roles support the larger organization. The complexity and detail included in an IT strategic plan should reflect the scale of the organization. Smaller IT departments, such as those operated by LTPAC organizations, may not benefit from a full-fledged plan.

Championing Culture

Culture, the way of life of a particular people, especially as shown in their ordinary behavior and habits, their attitudes towards each other, plays a critical role in the success of an organization. The values cited in a *value statement* should be present in the organization's culture. It is incumbent upon LTPAC IT leaders to champion the culture of their organization through their *presence* and *communications*.

1. *Presence*: Leaders reinforce the desired culture of the organization by "living out" the organizational values in front of their employees. This means getting out of the office on a regular basis and interacting with employees in their workspaces. Sometimes referred to as "leadership rounding" (MyRounding, n.d.), employees appreciate their leaders making efforts to be accessible and show interest in the work of their employees. Leaders reinforce the organization's culture by demonstrating a willingness to do menial tasks, coming into the facility at off-hours, and getting their hands dirty alongside their employees.

2. *Communications*: Written and oral communications are another way in which LTPAC IT leaders champion the organization's culture. Leaders need to ensure what they say as well as how they say things, aligns with the values of the organization. As employees and other stakeholders are continually assessing leaders based on their written and verbal communications, it is important leaders be purposeful in their communications.

There are two critical aspects of communication for every leader:

1. *Preparation*: Well-organized communications help recipients understand the goals and objectives for the information shared with them. Leaders need to spend the

appropriate time in outlining their thoughts and carefully weighing their words against the values of the organization. A good rule of thumb is to communicate such that anything the leader says is subject to evidentiary discovery in a court of law. With this understanding, leaders should not say anything that would embarrass their employer. Emotional reactive communications or inappropriate "jokes" have come back to haunt many leaders. A message template reinforcing the organization's values and brand can help keep leaders on message.

2. *Presentation:* Presentation and "presence" are different ideas. *Presentation* refers to the way in which one communicates. Speaking clearly, concisely, correctly, and with authority can reinforce the confidence people have in a leader. When giving a formal presentation, inform the audience upfront of the purpose and desired outcome of the presentation. During the presentation, have available all the information attendees need to understand, but be sure to only highlight the key points instead of every detail. When closing, restate both the purpose and the desired outcome and allow time to address questions and concerns. *Presentation* extends to formal and informal written communications. As the most senior representatives of the organization, leaders need to ensure their written communiqués are grammatically correct without spelling errors. This includes e-mails sent to other leaders as these e-mails can end up with those outside the intended audience.

Leadership Archetypes

How leaders leverage the two leadership functions discussed can largely determine the type of leader an individual will be. Manfred F. R. Kets de Vries, a well-respected scholar in the field of business leadership, in fact argues there are eight primary recurring patterns of behavior, or "archetypes," reflecting the various roles leaders can play in organization: (Kets de Vries, 2013)

1. *The strategist*: These people are good at dealing with developments in the organization's environment. They provide vision, strategic direction, and "outside-the-box" thinking to create new organizational forms and generate future growth.
2. *The change catalyst*: These executives love messy situations. They are masters at reengineering and creating new "organizational blueprints."
3. *The transactor*: These executives are great dealmakers. Skilled at identifying and tackling new opportunities, they thrive on negotiations.
4. *The builder*: These executives dream of creating something and have the talent and determination to make their dreams come true.
5. *The innovator*: These people focus on "the new." They possess a great capacity to solve extremely difficult problems.
6. *The processor*: These executives like organizations to be smoothly running, well-oiled machines. They are very effective at setting up the structures and systems needed to support an organization's objectives.
7. *The coach*: These executives know how to get the best out of people, thus creating high-performance cultures.
8. *The communicator*: These executives are great influencers, and have a considerable impact on their surroundings.

Leadership Guardrails

"Guardrails" exist to ensure LTPAC IT leaders stay focused on representing their organization appropriately. Three of the most significant guardrails follow.

Business Operations

LTPAC IT leaders are often part of the operational leadership of the entire organization. As such, they need to understand the organization's overall financial and budgetary reports, its comparative benchmarks, and its overall performance.

1. *Budgets*: To understand how the organization is doing financially, it is necessary to be able to read and understand a budget spreadsheet. Most often prepared by the company's financial leaders, IT leaders need to acquaint themselves with the annual budget by line item, to include the projected budget and expenditures to date. Variances between budgeted and actual expenditures to date are critical indicators suggesting business operations are not progressing as expected and therefore may require increased attention.
2. *Revenue and expenses*: Most healthcare organizations will project budget revenue and expenses by month as best as can be expected. While some expenses and revenues are easy to predict, measure, and compare, other expenditures and revenues have unique timing considerations that, if not understood, can lead to a false understanding of the business. A well-constructed budget report should include notations explaining the timing of events.
3. *Classification of expenses*: Most times, organizations treat IT hardware/software as an organizational asset because of its enduring value to the organization. Each asset depreciates over time at a fixed rate depending on the expected useful life of the asset. Depreciated expenses may show up in either IT or the operating department to which the asset belongs. Expenses that typically classify as "operating" include salaries, benefits, maintenance, travel, utilities, and supplies.
4. *Financial benchmarks*: Organizations frequently set goals for the following financial benchmarks:

- *Days in accounts receivable (AR)*: This is an expression of the average amount of time it takes organizations to receive payment from payers upon submission of the bills to the guarantor. Organizations will frequently set a goal for the number of days in AR.
- *Discharged not final billed (DNFB)*: This indicates the expected amount of money to bill the guarantor before submission of the final bill because of some outstanding documentation or procedural issue. AR and DFNB are important indicators because they represent outstanding money due to the organization.
- *Days cash on hand*: Represents the number of days the organization could continue to operate without receiving new funds. The larger the number, to a point, the better it is for the organization.

5. *Non-financial benchmarks*: External benchmarks may include additional financial indicators but are more likely to reflect healthcare quality, safety, regulatory, or accreditation measures.

Legal and Regulatory Compliance

The information and management systems industry includes a complex web of legal, regulatory, accreditation, and other compliance issues. Effective leaders need to understand the many nuances of these standards or to have easy access to individuals (e.g. a corporate compliance officer) who can assist in their understanding. Depending on the size of the organization, compliance responsibilities may all fall on the shoulders of one individual, though, most times an array of individuals around the organization have varied responsibilities. When dispersed, efforts of the responsible parties are frequently coordinated under the auspices of a corporate compliance committee, or perhaps an audit and education committee. Given the ever-changing nature of the information these individuals oversee, many organizations hire consultant firms to provide them with the most current information.

Business Ethics

Closely aligned with compliance is adherence to ethical business principles. Corporate financial implosions and evidence of legal and ethical impropriety have elevated the need for organizational and leadership ethics to be a topic of discussion in many companies. Adherence to an identifiable code of business or of corporate ethics is important to the practice of one's profession as well as modeling desired behaviors to one's staff.

Management

Understanding management concepts is vital for one to be an effective member of an organization's leadership team. Yet, given the enormous amount of information written on this topic, this chapter can only offer a brief synopsis of management principles. The following section divides management into the following three major areas:

1. Managing Operations
2. Managing Staff
3. Managing External Relationships

Managing Operations

Overseeing the operational activities of IT in an LTPAC facility should command the majority of the LTPAC IT manager's time. The present section groups the IT manager's operational duties into five broad categories:

1. IT strategic plan
2. IT budget
3. IT documentation

4. System performance
5. Managing projects

1. *IT strategic plan*: In order for the company to realize their goals, there is a need to translate the leader's vision and goals into specific action steps and tasks. Reflected in the organization's strategic plan, the strategic tasks contained in the strategic plan help managers and their staff remain focused on organizational priorities. The IT strategic plan ties to the organization's overall strategic plan. Central to the development of an IT strategic plan is the idea that there is no such thing as an "IT project." All projects are organizational and strategic in nature and IT is only one component of a bigger initiative. Once top managers understand and agree to this idea, they will recognize why every major initiative not only needs operational leadership sponsorship but the input of organizational leaders as well as of staff directly responsible for the following actionable components.
   - *Strategic map*: A well-developed plan will map the organizational strategies and the supporting applications and processes for each strategy. Once fully developed, the *strategic map* acts as visual representation of the current systems' statuses, an indicator of the expected useful lifetime of the systems, and a depiction of the gap existing between the strategy and the needed technology.
   - *Gap analysis*: The plan's *gap analysis* outlines areas where disconnects between the current IT systems and processes and the desired future state exist. Managers use the gap analysis to identify potential processes and system changes that could bridge the gap. In cases where the gap requires multiple processes or system changes, the plan needs to outline the steps that can achieve the desired outcome. As many of the identified steps may take years to complete, the plan's details

need only focus on those steps that relate to the first year or two of the plan.

- *IT-specific efforts*: If warranted, the IT plan should include some of the more IT-specific initiatives (e.g. updating computer monitors) and IT personnel needs (e.g. adding staff to the help desk). This section of the plan considers current and future resourcing needs as well as transition and succession plans for staff.

The IT strategic plan is a "living document" once it is created. To achieve this, the document needs to be included in the organizational strategic plan with updates made as changes occur. Key IT objectives should be visible to all IT employees so they have an opportunity to see and commit to each objective on a daily basis. Tying individual performance objectives to the plan is an effective way of ensuring the staff keep the IT strategic plan at the top of their minds. Key to a successful implementation of the IT strategic plan is ensuring stakeholders clearly understand technological opportunities and constraints. IT champions must assist stakeholders in understanding where automation tools can help, as well as tempering any unrealistic expectations.

2. *IT budget*: As a significant and growing cost center in an LTPAC organization, IT managers should have at least a working knowledge of basic financial operations to include budgeting and planning; financial purchasing options; operating expenses; basic accounting principles and standards; financial models and methods; and compliance regulations. Managing budgets is one of the basic disciplines that all managers must master. An organized approach to developing and maintaining the budget will go a long way in helping reduce budget risk.

3. *IT documentation*: Documentation involving the IT system and IT activities is critical. As a communication tool, documentation allows for a continuity of effort independent of the "knowledge" any one individual in the

organization. While documentation efforts cover a wide array of areas and activities within the facility, IT documentation groups as follows:

- *System documentation*: System documentation focuses on any information involving the overall IT system, to include:
  - *system selection* (documents supporting analysis, decision-making, and acquisition)
  - *system implementation*
  - *system features, functionalities, and technical requirements*
  - *system analysis* (documents involving information system (IS) requirements and the environment in which the system will operate) and *operating manuals*

- *Operational documentation*: Operational documentation mostly relates to ongoing systems operations and maintenance. This type of information involves documentation of the ongoing testing of systems and results, of audit processes and database management, as well as including training manuals. Operational documents can also encompass implementation timeframes, flow charts, and progress reports; data backup and recovery procedures; and system retirement, tuning, and logistic support requirements.

- *Department documentation*: Department policies and procedures (P&P) documents help guide the processes and actions that employees use to perform their work. Policies and procedures serve related but different purposes. Both types of documents set performance requirements to help motivate and discipline employees, as well as serving as ongoing references for employees and orientation documents for new hires. *Policy documents* formalize what is expected or required of employees whereas *procedure documents* describe how to accomplish an outcome. P&Ps are essential for many healthcare organizations such as LTPAC facilities to achieve various accreditations.

4. *System performance*: Simply stated, IT managers are responsible for ensuring the organization's IT system works and is reliable. Managers must therefore set clear expectations, or a plan, for the type of information they manage, the system's quality standards, and a defined performance improvement process. The following section focuses on efforts to evaluate the system's performance.

   – *Baseline assessment*: A baseline assessment provides managers with data on how stakeholders are using the system and their expectations of the system. IT managers can conduct a baseline assessment in one of several ways (face-to-face interviews; actual observation of the system in use, etc.) with the most efficient approach being group meetings focused on examining specific situations. During these meetings, managers will want to understand the stakeholders' expectations of system availability and performance paying close attention to any references to negative changes in system performance. As stakeholders will often cite opportunities for system improvements during these meetings, managers should let stakeholders know that the accommodation of all improvement requests is unlikely. Once the baseline is determined, managers should commit to a regular process of follow-up analyses. If the organization agrees that the performance of IT systems and services is satisfactory, then an annual follow-up assessment may suffice. A lower than desirable assessment warrants a prompt response and more frequent follow-up. Regular communication or monthly reports should address commitments to improvement.

   – *Software evaluation*: One area IT managers most frequently need to address in assessing the system's performance surrounds the software used by the facility.

Software quality assurance begins with the staff that implements and configures the software. Performance testing results are provided by the software vendors themselves and internally developed quality assurance scripts.

- *Technical and information needs recommendations*: As clinical IT managers gain a better understanding of the system's performance, they are in a position to make recommendations surrounding the organization's technical and information needs. It is important that all organizational leaders understand that operational goals direct information technology and not the reverse. For this reason, information management and system leaders need to be keenly aware of organizational goals and recommend appropriate systems and technologies in support of those goals if called upon. Organizations that stay focused on goals will not catch the IT leader off guard. When goal deviation does occur, the IT leader needs to be ready to challenge the request to deviate from organizational goals and be prepared to collect appropriate supporting materials to attend to the updated goals.

5. *Managing projects*: Another major role of the IT manager involves project management. Project management is the discipline of planning, organizing, securing, managing, leading, and controlling resources to achieve specific goals. A project is a temporary activity in that it has a defined beginning and end. The temporary nature of projects stands in contrast with organizational operational initiatives, which consist of repetitive, permanent, or semi-permanent functional activities. LTPAC organizations use the project management methodology to implement new and complex IT systems. In cases where multiple interdependent projects exist, program management manages all of the projects as a group.

The project manager is critical to the successful conclusion of projects. The project manager is responsible for working with project sponsors, the project team, and others involved in the project to meet project goals and deliver the project within budget and on schedule. The project manager controls project resources to best meet project objectives; manage project scope, schedule, and cost; report on project progress; and facilitate and resolve issues, conflicts, risks, and other obstacles to project success.

Communication plays a significant role in the success of a project. IT Managers need to ensure a project has and follows a communication plan. For project communications, the timeline and the completion status are the best first materials for review. In a project status report, a color-coded summary of tasks and statuses provides valuable visual clues.

In today's complex healthcare environment, steering committees are essential in providing guidance and practical direction for IT project and operational initiatives. A steering committee is an advisory committee, usually made up of high-level stakeholders and/or experts. These individuals provide guidance on key issues such as a company's policy and objectives, budgetary control, marketing strategy, resource allocation, and decisions involving large expenditures. IT steering committees are a best-practice approach in healthcare organizations for aligning strategic business and IT priorities. Steering committees, which usually include executives and departmental heads, focus on three main tasks:

– IT strategic planning
– Project prioritization
– Project approval

Clear mandates and a real ability to influence decision-making through executive participation increase the value of IT steering committees.

To form an effective IT steering committee and keep it on track, managers should consider the following:

a. *Ensure IT priorities align with strategic business priorities*: Focus on core IT steering objectives and not IT resource allocation, as well as on stress-shared decision-making and fostering a culture of communication between business units.

b. *Develop a steering committee charter*: It should outline the key tasks and responsibilities of the committee.

c. *Keep the IT steering committee small and schedule regular meetings*: Ensuring that the membership is consistently informed, engaged as needed on the project scope and timelines, and that it includes executive decision-making authority is critical to the success of the IT steering committee.

During the life of a project, new opportunities occasionally pop up. A disciplined analysis following the project planning approach will weigh the merits of new opportunities in the context of the project as a whole. If a value-added suggestion is made and approved, then the plan should be amended and the appropriate communications undertaken. A well-written, approved plan will help to eliminate the opportunity for "scope creep" to infiltrate the project, a common event in the life of a project. *Scope creep* is the undisciplined addition of new goals, objectives, and milestones that may have a negative effect on the cost or timeline of a project. This occurs when inadequate analyses of suggestions work their way into the process. An effective way of eliminating scope creep is to anticipate it and have a method of reviewing recommended changes in scope with the project's leadership team on a regular basis.

Managing Staff

The increased adoption of technology in healthcare has expanded the role of IT. In addition to traditional or general

IT functions, the field of healthcare IT has created new roles and responsibilities.

1. *IT roles*: Roles and responsibilities within healthcare IT can be broken down into the following categories:
   - *Senior management roles and responsibilities*: Board of director, executive management, and medical executive committee support are essential for the success of IT in a healthcare organization. The chief information officer (CIO) is generally the most senior-level IT executive. In many health systems, this role also carries the vice president or senior vice president designation. Today's CIO is fully involved in the organization's internal and external clinical technology operations. The CIO typically reports to the CEO and is a consultant to the CEO and executive staff on what newer technology can bring to the successful clinical operations of the provider. Additional IT-related leadership roles can include the chief medical information officer (CMIO), the chief nursing information officer (CNIO), the chief technology officer (CTO), the chief information security officer (CISO), IT department directors, the chief project officer, and physician and nurse champions. Recently, health systems have developed new roles, such as the chief innovation officer, chief applications officer, and chief privacy officer to meet the evolving technology environment.
   - *General IT roles and responsibilities*: Healthcare organization IT departments are staffed with internal full-time employees and/or outsourced staff that support traditional IT-related roles. Job descriptions for these roles collapse into senior level, mid-level, and junior level, and typically include titles such as director, manager, architect, analyst, engineer, technician, administrator, programmer, and developer. Common fields that these roles cover are applications, business

intelligence, data warehousing, databases, data centers, directory services, help-desk services, IT security, mobile applications, servers, networks, telecommunications, storage, systems integration, backup, messaging, collaboration, technical documentation, virtualization, and web presence.

– *Healthcare IT roles and responsibilities*: To meet the evolving technology demands of healthcare organizations, particularly in light of the increased usage of electronic health records (EHRs), many clinical, business, and project-related roles now require healthcare IT knowledge and a blend of clinical, management, and technical experience. Some of the more in-demand clinical and business positions are analyst roles. These include specialty roles covering systems, administrative support, applications, clinical systems, reports, finance, supply chains, human resources and payroll, revenue cycles, decision support, interfaces, and business intelligence. Other important healthcare IT roles have positions in informatics, clinical engineering, go-live events, implementation consulting, integration, project management, quality assurance, and usability.

– *EHR roles and responsibilities*: The U.S. Office of the National Coordinator for Health Information Technology identified the following six healthcare IT workforce roles healthcare organizations will need to fill as they deploy EHRs: (ONC, 2010)

1. *Practice workflow/information management redesign specialist*: Workers in this role assist in reorganizing the work of a provider to take full advantage of the features of healthcare IT to improve health and care.

2. *Implementation manager*: Workers in this role provide on-site management of mobile adoption support teams before and during implementation of

healthcare IT systems in clinical and public health settings.

3. *Implementation support specialist*: Workers in this role provide on-site user support during implementation of healthcare IT systems in clinical and public health settings. These individuals will provide support services complementing those provided by the vendor to be sure the technology functions properly and meets the needs of the redesigned practice workflow.

4. *Clinician/practitioner consultant*: This role is similar to the practice workflow/information management redesign specialist, but brings to bear the background and experience of a licensed clinician or public health professional.

5. *Software support technician*: Workers in this role maintain systems in clinical and public health settings, including the patching and upgrading of software. They also provide one-on-one support in a traditional help-desk model to individual users with questions or problems.

6. *Trainer*: Workers in this role use adult learning principles to design and deliver training programs to employees in clinical and public health settings

2. *Employee development*: Employee development is a key component in ensuring healthcare IT staff attain competency in information and management system tools and skills. Mastering those skills, along with the "soft skills" needed to collaborate and work together as a team, is essential in ensuring the success of the organization. Staff improvement programs provide employees with the proficiencies and qualifications needed for advancement within the organization, and help staff form attitudes and interpersonal skills to work effectively. Employee development is available through training and in-service

programs, certification classes, community college or university educational courses, conferences and workshops, professional association involvement, and self-study through books, industry magazines, videos, and online resources.

– *Training and in-service programs*: Training and in-service programs may originate from several sources. The human resources department typically has responsibility for organization-wide training requirements, such as security and safety regulations, discriminatory practices, and quality improvements. The department or group in which an employee works provides programs such as in-service or line training. In addition, IT projects for information and management system deployments usually include a training budget for system developers, administrators, and end users who will be supporting and using the product.

– *IT-based certifications*: IT-based certifications have long been a mainstay of IT education and professional credentials. Certifications have two main advantages. First, they provide a framework by which technical staff can learn and gain a level of proficiency in a specific IT-related topic. Second, a certification provides the recipients with a credential showing they understand a defined body of knowledge in a specific area. Although a certification by itself will not qualify a person for a new job or promotion, it does demonstrate that the individual has mastered the basic level of a specific knowledge area, and is a positive contributing factor in the decision of whom to hire. Clinicians are encouraged to keep their clinical licensure and certifications active and up-to-date, even if they are no longer in a clinical role. IT professionals should also consider keeping their IT certifications active, particularly those certifications that are in high demand in healthcare IT.

– *Healthcare IT certifications*: The Certified Professional in Healthcare Information and Management Systems (CPHIMS) certification is an essential credential for all healthcare IT management, management engineering and process improvement professionals, U.S. military personnel, and consultants. It is the only credential sponsored by a healthcare IT professional association, and eligible candidates become certified by passing the challenging CPHIMS exam. The CPHIMS certification verifies that individuals have the knowledge necessary to be successful in healthcare IT. A CPHIMS is a member of an elite group of healthcare professionals with demonstrated expertise in the important categories of healthcare and technology environments, IT systems, leadership, and management. In addition, the Certified Association in Healthcare Information and Management Systems (CAHIMS) is an entry-level credential designed to serve as a career pathway to the CPHIMS. Unlike the CPHIMS, there are no experiential requirements, only a high school diploma or the equivalent, and the willingness to sit for a rigorous exam that covers introductory healthcare IT content. Many of today's highly sought-after healthcare IT certifications are available only to employees of organizations that are engaged in a specific vendor product deployment, such as an EHR or healthcare information systems project. However, healthcare systems also value generally available certifications, particularly if they are in the process of deploying related methodologies throughout their organization. These include certifications such as the Project Management Professional, Information Technology Infrastructure Library, and Lean Six Sigma.

– *Other professional development*: Healthcare IT professionals should also consider other professional development and education opportunities. These are particularly useful in helping individuals remain current in the rapidly evolving healthcare environment. Employees are typically responsible for the costs of their professional development, but many companies pay for such education as a benefit of employment. The overall education of the IT team members extends beyond the applications they service and the immediate issues and objectives that are at hand. Team members need to stay connected to a variety of disciplines related to their specific sphere of expertise. The greatest opportunity for this added education comes from within the organization itself. IT managers should encourage their staff to listen to the expertise of their colleagues and peers.

3. *Performance evaluation*: Performance evaluation is an important tool a manager should utilize to monitor and improve employee competency. Performance evaluations involve assessments of the employees' work, outcomes, attitudes and interpersonal skills, professional growth, and adherence to organizational values, as well as feedback to the employee. Some believe performance evaluations are important only to employees who are performing at a less-than-satisfactory level. However, performance evaluations are just as important in helping highly effective employees maintain their level of performance.

   The evaluation process involves a comparison of an employee's actual and expected performance. In order to be effective, the performance evaluation process must start with clearly measurable performance goals. A variety of methods can be used in the performance evaluation process with the most common being a rating scale. Scales specify personal traits and the behaviors expected, such as teamwork, communication skills, dependability, and initiative. Also specified will be job attributes such as the quality and quantity of work.

   In the performance appraisal process, it is important for the manager to provide feedback to employees at regular intervals during the evaluation year. This way, employees will not be surprised with a less-than-adequate performance review. In addition, it gives them the opportunity to improve their performance. Alternatively, if an employee is performing at an excellent or exceptional level, the interim positive feedback will help to preserve that positive behavior. Although interim reviews can be done formally or informally, it is advisable to complete a formal interim review if an employee's performance requires improvement.

Disciplinary action, if needed, relies on clear facts and with documented justification. Disciplinary action should be done progressively over time starting with verbal discussions, progressing to written and verbal communications, and if required, ending in termination. This approach provides consistent communication to the employee about problem areas. Communication may be oral at first. If the problem persists, documentation is appropriate and should be included in the form of notes to the employee's record. At all steps in the process, it is advisable to communicate with and seek the advice of human resources.

Managing External Relationships

The third major area IT managers oversee involves "external relationships." External parties of interest are *vendors* and *customers*.

1. *Vendors*: IT managers are increasingly turning to vendors for the expertise and support they need to meet the technology requirements of their organizations. The reliance on vendor partnerships has enabled vendors to play a key role in the success of many healthcare organizations. Vendor management is not simply negotiating the lowest price possible. It involves working with vendors

on contract performance, schedules and costs, product functionality, and support and maintenance agreements. The vendor management process begins with selecting the right vendor for the right reasons. The contract identifies the restrictions or exclusions, with penalties and terms being beneficial to both parties. Once the relationship with the vendor has begun, it is important to monitor vendor performance, with particular attention to the requirements that are most critical to the healthcare organization. Regular communication between the vendor and the healthcare organization will help to avoid misunderstandings and address issues before they become problems.

2. *Customers*: Healthcare is primarily a people business and it demands that the organization be particularly customer-focused, or customer-centric. There are several specific factors and approaches to consider in organizing the customer-service functions in the IT department.

 – *Service-Level Agreement (SLA)*: Because IT departments undertake many tasks, service-level agreements (SLAs) are important as a reference to service obligations. Ideally, every service request the IT department receives includes an SLA documenting the specific levels of service expected and the evaluation metrics.

 – *Request tracking*: In managing an SLA, the IT department will need to implement a request-tracking process involving the following:

 • *Help-desk triage*: A process for assigning priority levels to requests.
 • *Issue tracking*: The ongoing monitoring of open, new, and closed service requests.
 • *User satisfaction surveys*: Distributed upon the completion of a service, users respond to a satisfaction survey assessing how well the provider met the service objectives.

3. *Help desk*: The most measured IT area is usually the help desk. A key measure of effectiveness is the *first-call resolution rate*, the percentage of service requests that are resolved during the initial call to the service technician. Another help-desk measure is the *call-abandonment rate*, the percentage of times callers hang up without speaking to a technician. If the average wait times are high, the call-abandonment rate will probably be high as well. The longer callers wait, the more likely they are to give up.

Summary

With the increased adoption of healthcare IT, there are a myriad of new roles and responsibilities developing within general IT, healthcare IT, and IT management. Managers are looking to ensure that their staff members are properly trained and educated. Today's leaders require a blend of clinical awareness—experience in operational, financial, and project management—and technical knowledge to be successful. Healthcare organizations are increasingly turning to vendors and consultants for the expertise and support they need to meet their IT requirements. Stakeholder management using effective steering committees, the implementation of industry best practices, and experience with well-defined customer service processes are important requirements for healthcare administrators. By maintaining appropriate documentation, giving careful attention to financial and budget risks, and managing customer relationships, healthcare organizations will continue to experience success.

For Discussion

1. Discuss the differences, if any, between IT leaders and IT managers.

2. Describe how individuals and organizations benefit from shared value systems.
3. Explain how IT leaders take to envision the future of their organization.
4. Relate some actions that an IT leader can take to create a climate for change and encourage risk-taking. Be specific.
5. Illustrate methods that IT leaders use to instill confidence in the people they are leading.

References

English Oxford Living Dictionaries. (n.d.). Strategy. Retrieved from English Oxford Living Dictionaries: https://en.oxforddictionaries.com/definition/strategy

Kets de Vries, M. F. (2013, December 18). The Eight Archetypes of Leadership. Retrieved from Harvard Business Review: https://hbr.org/2013/12/the-eight-archetypes-of-leadership

Kotter, J. P. (2013, January 13). Management Is (Still) Not Leadership. Retrieved from Harvard Business Review: https://hbr.org/2013/01/management-is-still-not-leadership

MyRounding. (n.d.). Leadership Rounding. Retrieved from MyRounding: http://www.myrounding.com/the-application/leadership-rounding

ONC. (2010, June 3). Health IT Workforce Roles and Competencies Categories of Health IT Workforce Roles Requiring Short-Term Training. Retrieved from ONC: https://www.healthit.gov/sites/default/files/health-it-workforce-6-month-roles-as-of-06-03-10.pdf

OTHER CONSIDERATIONS

Chapter 7

LTPAC and Future Considerations

Learning Objectives

Reading this chapter will enable you to

- State the relationship of LTPAC to the Quadruple Aim.
- Describe characteristics and potential outcomes of person-centered models of care.
- Define the five Valued Quality Coordination of Care (VQCC) Differentials.

Introduction

Projecting the future of health IT in the LTPAC provider market is a difficult task. To begin with, healthcare is a complex industry. As detailed in the first chapter of this textbook, the healthcare ecosystem presents as highly fragmented resulting in a system that suffers from a lack of coordination, high variability in outcomes, and a failure to tie costs to quality. With the current system appearing as unsustainable, perhaps the most assured projection one can make is that the current system will have to change.

The task of projecting the future of health IT in the LTPAC provider market becomes harder when recognizing the dynamic nature of the industry. A prime example of the changing nature of the healthcare ecosystem is evident in efforts to define the aim of healthcare. In 2008, the future director of CMS wrote a paper addressing the three primary aims of healthcare in the United States. Referred to as the "Triple Aim of Healthcare," these recommendations became the cornerstone strategy for *improving quality of care,* the *health of populations,* and *reduced costs* in the United States:

> Improving the U.S. health care system requires simultaneous pursuit of three aims: improving the experience of care, improving the health of populations, and reducing per capita costs of health care. Preconditions for this include the enrollment of an identified population, a commitment to universality for its members, and the existence of an organization (an "integrator") that accepts responsibility for all three aims for that population. The integrator's role includes at least five components: partnership with individuals and families, redesign of primary care, population health management, financial management, and macro system integration.

> **(Berwick, Nolan, & Whittington, 2008)**

As an array of healthcare stakeholders began to focus on achieving the three aims, a consensus emerged that a fourth aim, the *well-being of the care team,* was required. The introduction of the fourth aim has become an important strategy to improve healthcare service performance, prevent burnout, and improve the lives of personnel in the healthcare workforce:

The Triple Aim—enhancing patient experience, improving population health, and reducing costs— is widely accepted as a compass to optimize health system performance. Yet physicians and other members of the healthcare workforce report widespread burnout and dissatisfaction. Burnout is associated with lower patient satisfaction, reduced health outcomes, and it may increase costs. Burnout thus imperils the Triple Aim. This article recommends that the Triple Aim be expanded to a Quadruple Aim, adding the goal of improving the work life of health care providers, including clinicians and staff.

(Bodenheimer & Sinsky, 2014)

While the challenges just noted complicate efforts to project the future, the exercise to do so is valuable nonetheless. Forward-looking efforts help those within the industry to "skate to where the puck is going to be." To get a sense of the future of health IT in the LTPAC provider market, it is important to explore significant trends influencing the worlds of digital health and the LTPAC industry. While by no means an exhaustive list of the array of forces affecting these areas, the following chapter considers two significant trends:

1. Person-centered care models
2. Longitudinal health records

Before diving into the potential impact these trends may have on LTPAC provider organizations, it is essential to establish a baseline understanding of the unique value LTPAC provider organizations offer the healthcare ecosystem. Once established, the reader is better equipped to consider how LTPAC organizations may respond to the aforementioned trends.

Valued Quality Coordination of Care

Perhaps one of the most comprehensive summaries of the distinct value LTPAC provider organizations offer the market came from the LTPAC Health IT Collaborative (Derr, 2016). Spurred on by Karen DeSalvo, MD, then Director of the Office of the National Coordinator for Health Information Technology and Deputy Secretary of HHS, the Collaborative developed a Brief for ONC detailing the unique characteristics LTPAC provider organizations offer the marketplace. Referred to as the *Valued Quality Coordination of Care* (VQCC) *Differentials*, the VQCC lists five unique value propositions or "differentials" that highlight how LTPAC's holistic approach to care benefits the individual.

VQCC #1: Duration of Care

Perhaps the most obvious differential involves the length of time patients are under the care of a provider organization. In comparison to hospitals where the average length of stay (LOS) is in days, by definition a person under the care of an LTPAC provider organization can stay for weeks, months, or even years. This extended period of time afforded to LTPAC provider organizations is invaluable to developing, implementing, and maintaining the person's care plan over an extended time. In many cases, LTPAC provider organizations are the first care settings that can develop a comprehensive holistic chronic care longitudinal plan of care that takes into consideration all aspects of care, to include:

- eAssessment of the person's total health condition
- Evaluation of the person's health leading up to an acute hospitalization
- Necessary long-term rehabilitation therapy
- Chronic care conditions and possible comorbidities

- Psychosocial and behavioral health concerns
- Medication management including polypharmacy
- Familial relations and interactions
- Education on adjusting to a new quality-of-life situation when returning home

VQCC #2: eAssessments

LTPAC provider organizations have an extensive history of using digital technologies to report on the clinical assessments of the persons under their care. Nursing facilities, for example, have submitted Minimum Data Set (MDS) assessments electronically to CMS for a number of years in order to receive payment for the care delivered. In accordance to CMS regulations, LTPAC provider organizations conduct a comprehensive eAssessment for each patient they receive from a hospital, routinely throughout a person's stay in the facility, as well as when there is a change in a person's clinical state.

VQCC #3: Chronic Care Comorbidity Care

There is perhaps no population of patients who can benefit more from chronic care management than those residing in LTPAC settings. Long-term residents of nursing facilities, for example, typically have multiple chronic conditions, and dedicated nursing staff, caregivers, and practitioners are in a position to provide sound management for this frail population. While acute care providers are aware of a person's possible chronic care conditions, their primary focus is mainly on addressing episodic disease conditions. As such, acute care providers tend to focus on mortality and readmission outcomes whereas LTPAC providers focus on functional mobility and activities of daily living (ADL) outcomes. One of the major LTPAC differentials then is the ability and experience of staff to conduct comprehensive person-centric assessments of the persons under their care.

VQCC #4: Medication Management

Polypharmacy, the use of multiple medications by an individual, is common among persons under the care of an LTPAC provider organization. Some have even suggested that up to half of nursing home residents, use nine or more drugs. The multiplicity of medications in use increases the potential for negative patient outcomes. Given the propensity for and challenge of polypharmacy in LTPAC settings, LTPAC provider organizations have a medication team to conduct comprehensive integrated person-centric management of medications. These teams also function to provide medication counseling when transitioning persons to another provider or home.

VQCC #5: Technology

The fifth and final differentiator centers on the unique technologies used in LTPAC settings. A myriad of new technologies has been developed to support LTPAC patients and is being expanded by LTPAC providers as this healthcare segment invests millions of dollars in the future healthcare system. The technologies designed to address the specific needs of the LTPAC patient include:

- Clinical IT technology
- Therapy technology
- Telehealth and remote patient monitoring (RPM) technology
- Telemedicine and physician consultation technology
- Medication management technology
- Social technology

The five VQCCs are important in the transitions of care between a hospital and an SNF. As an example, a hospital accepts a person who requires surgery. The acute hospital conducts a presurgical assessment on the person receiving surgery. Typically, these abbreviated assessments are not as holistic, as they only consider chronic care conditions as they affect the upcoming surgery. Post-surgery, when the person transitions to an SNF, services are mainly for surgical recovery or rehabilitation. When an SNF accepts this person, they conduct a full standard holistic assessment. Many times this holistic assessment discovers chronic conditions that were not included in the post-surgery transitions of care document (Stoicea et al., 2017). The SNF has to expand the person's diagnosis, care, maintenance, and future care plan due to this information gap.

Future Trends

Having established a baseline understanding of the unique characteristics LTPAC provider organizations offer the health-care ecosystem, the reader is equipped to understand how the following market trends may affect LTPAC provider organizations.

Person-Centered Models

In 2001, the Institute of Medicine identified "patient-centered care" as one of the six pillars of quality healthcare, describing it as: "providing care that is respectful of and responsive to individual patient preferences, needs, and values, and ensuring that patient values guide all clinical decisions"(IOM, 2001).

While the traditional term or title for an individual receiving care is "patient," in recent years "person" has become the core concept guiding the philosophical change from a traditional medical model to a more humanistic approach to medical care

(Li & Porock, 2014). As such, readers are encouraged to adopt the term "person-centered care" in place of the dated term "patient-centered care."

Person-centric care is not a new healthcare concept. In the 1980s, person-centered care approaches were most evident in behavioral health settings where there was a concern for ensuring a safe psychological environment within which people could move towards greater self-awareness and better fulfillment of their potential (Rogers, 1980). A groundbreaking book, *Through the Patients Eyes* (Gerteis, Edgman-Levitan, Daley, & Delbanco, 1993), suggests two predominant criteria about person-centered care. First, care must be rooted in a person's subjective illness experience. To deal only with objectively defined illness criteria, such as peripheral vascular circulation or fall risk, is not enough. Second, persons receiving healthcare, and clinicians involved in a person's care, have a shared responsibility to define the care plan together (Suchman, 1994). These early criteria were precursors to the following eight foundational principles recommended for person-centered care, frequently referred to now as The Eight Picker Principals of Patient-Centered Care (Picker, n.d.). These eight core principles, descriptions, and applications (OneView, 2015) are illustrated in Figure 7.1.

> *Principle 1: Respect for a person's values, preferences, and needs.* A person receiving healthcare services has their own set of values and core beliefs, which influence their decisions about healthcare. Healthcare providers have a duty then to treat persons with dignity and respect by paying attention to these values and core beliefs during important decisions. For example, under Provision 1 of the American Nurse Association's Code of Ethics, professional nurses in practice are obligated to:
> – Respect and treat persons with dignity.
> – Develop trusting relationships.

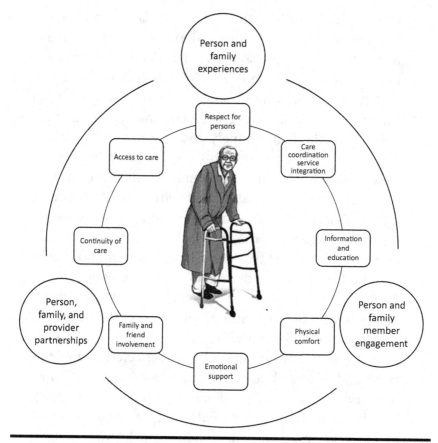

Figure 7.1   Principles of person-centered care and measurable outcomes. (Design by R. Pagenkopp.)

- Set aside bias and prejudice in helping people make decisions.
- Have open and honest dialogue so that persons understand what is happening to them.
- Allow people their moral and legal right to choose what is to happen to their person once they understand their situation.
- Prevent harm by fostering safety in a person's environment (Winland-Brown, Lachman, & O'Connor Swanson, 2015).

Principle 2: Care Coordination and Integration of Services.
Proper care coordination and integration of services help

alleviate a person's feelings of vulnerability and power-lessness. Proper care coordination assumes that a person's needs have been assessed and that deliberate actions are planned to meet those needs, including organizing patient care activities, sharing information with appropriate persons involved in the care, and planning appropriate care delivery methods in a timely and safe manner to reach desired goals of care. Health IT is a broad mechanism used to maximize care coordination activities (AHRQ, 2016). For example, health IT systems provide a means by which to classify the activities that are widely used by professional care coordinators (e.g. communication and managing activities) that assist in developing more effective models of care coordination (Popejoy et al., 2015).

Principle 3: Information and Education. Healthcare providers have a duty to inform persons seeking healthcare about their condition and treatment plan so they are knowledgeable about their illness, expected treatment plan, and potential outcomes. Accurate, timely information and education can reduce anxiety and fears about healthcare delivery. Additionally, a knowledgeable person may be more autonomous in their decision-making about their healthcare situation. Reciprocal relationships that include the sharing of information and knowledge between healthcare providers and persons under their care are important to help understand contextual and environmental variables that may affect care delivery. For example, gaps in information and knowledge occur between when a person's illness starts and when a healthcare provider becomes involved in treating their illness (Alexander, 2007). Understanding the actions taken by a person with an illness prior to the time they encountered a healthcare professional is vital to the actions that a provider decides to take to alleviate symptoms.

Principle 4: Physical Comfort. A person's physical comfort level is crucially important in their overall experience.

Physical comfort is associated with the experience of pain and difficulty performing regular activities of daily living. Resident-centered outcomes used in person-centered care intervention research have shown some positive results. To illustrate, some person-centered interventions found a lower percentage of residents who were dependent in eating (Chang, Li, & Porock, 2013).

Principle 5: Emotional Support. Particular pathways exist where social support systems link with improved health outcomes. Operationalized in a multiplicity of ways, emotional support systems exist in the different types of transactions occurring between persons (Reblin & Uchino, 2008). Personal transactions leading to greater perceived emotional support have impacts on health outcomes. For example, one study found the discrepancy between perceived and received support predicted mortality in dialysis patients (Lyyra & Heikkinen, 2006). Caregivers should pay particular attention to a person's support systems. Low levels of perceived support can produce increased anxiety levels not only in the person receiving the care, but also in their caregivers.

The delivery of emotional support through electronic healthcare transactions is becoming more common in LTPAC settings. One case in point includes secure online websites, which provide people 24-h access to personal health information, as long as there is an internet connection (ONC, 2015). These websites allow persons to interact with their healthcare team, enhancing emotional support in a variety of ways, such as exchanging health information, requesting prescriptions, scheduling non-urgent appointments, and viewing educational materials. These interactive features intend to engage persons in their own healthcare by encouraging a more active role in the daily management and monitoring of their health conditions. Though the prevalence of these technologies is increasing, there is still a paucity of evidence of their effectiveness. This is especially true in LTPAC settings where the adoption of health IT has lagged (Kruse, Mileski, Alaytsev, Carol, & Williams, 2015). Some evidence suggests both positive and negative outcomes to the use of this technology (Kruse, Argueta, Lopez, & Nair, 2015). The affinity of patients and providers with using this technology is mixed. Most concerns involve the secureness of messaging, improved quality and disease outcomes, the availability of educational resources, user friendliness, costs, and timeliness.

Principle 6: Involvement of Friends and Family. The role family and friends play in a person's illness trajectory are crucial for that person's healthcare experience. These roles incorporate a person's family and their representative in healthcare decisions (when appropriate) to ensure the person's needs and desires are met. Friends and family are involved in the care of a loved one through a continuum of consultation and/or partnerships with the healthcare team. The use of electronic health records (EHR) introduces some subtle shifts in the roles of friends and family along this continuum. At one end of the spectrum, clinicians use printouts from clinical laboratory reports in the EHR to discuss the health status of a person. In this scenario, persons in an LTPAC setting do not interact with the EHR but rely on healthcare providers for information. At the midpoint of the continuum, a person can use the EHR to access clinical laboratory reports, but they are not able to correct or contribute additional information. At the other end of the continuum, partnerships develop whereby a person can access medical records, is able to see clinical data, and can edit or change their personal health information (Carman et al., 2013). Person-centered trajectories involving family and friends might consider the types of accommodation available to facilitate the proximity of loved ones, involving loved ones in decisions, and recognize the needs of loved ones early on and support these needs.

Principle 7: Continuity and Transition. The ability of a
person to remain healthy, active, and independent as
long as possible is a crucial part of the healthcare planning process. Incorporating resources that can facilitate
this outcome is important as a person transitions from
one healthcare setting to another. Required resources
for appropriate person-centered care activities during
transitions may address issues related to medication
management, physical limitations, dietary requirements, environmental monitoring for safety, and others. Ongoing education about access to clinical care,
social services, therapy for rehabilitation, and financial
well-being is also necessary. Health IT plays a vital role
in the sharing of information and educating persons
about their healthcare, involving a person's family and
family representatives in care activities, and the healthcare team. For example, health information exchanges
used to securely share clinical data from the EHR as
care transitions occur between settings are becoming
more widespread in long-term care services (Abramson,
McGinnis, Moore, Kaushal, & Investigators, 2014;
Yeaman, 2015). Six non-urgent situations where health
information exchange is most valuable in person-centric
care transitions from/to nursing homes, for instance,
include

1. Scheduling appointments
2. Laboratory specimen drawing
3. Pharmacy orders and reconciliation
4. Social work discharge planning
5. Admissions and pre-admissions, and
6. Pharmacy-medication reconciliation (Alexander et al.,
   2015)

The most important issues raised by staff who are implementing these technologies in nursing homes is the
availability of information technology in clinical settings, accessibility of health information exchange

at the point-of-care, and policies/procedures for sending/receiving secure personal health information (Alexander et al., 2015).

Principle 8: Access to Care. Persons requiring ongoing care need to know how to access care. Furthermore, a person-centered approach should emphasize factors affecting a person's ability to access care, such as their proximity to facilities and services, available transportation, ability to schedule appointments, and how to get referrals to specialists if needed. Successfully adopting health IT and incorporating recommendations from the previous seven guiding principles will facilitate greater access to care, which is an important measure used to assess person-centered care.

Person-Centered Outcome Measures

Person- and family-centered outcome measures are high priorities for future consideration in LTPAC settings (NQF, 2017). Leaders interested in person-centric models of care have identified several factors that facilitate the degree of person-centered engagement. These factors include the person's type of involvement during patient-centered care activities, the role of the person including family, the person receiving care, and provider, as well as environmental variables (Hetland, McAndrew, Perazzo, & Hickman, 2017). Factors associated with the family are time and extent of involvement and presence during care delivery. Increased family time and involvement in care delivery activities prepares families for emotionally volatile situations, increases their understanding of interventions, prepares them for risks, and helps them understand healthcare provider roles during the delivery of healthcare services. Factors facilitating person-centered care include decreased anxiety or fear towards family care. Anxiety and fear are especially reduced when persons receiving care have a positive response to family involvement in care decisions, such as when determining the severity of illness, neurological status changes, or when lines, tubes, or equipment are being used during patient care.

Person-Centered Partnership Measures

Partnership outcomes may include the frequency of documentation of a durable power of attorney by a caregiver responsible for care delivery and the subsequent availability of that documentation in the person's electronic health records (Galambos, Starr, Rantz, & Petroski, 2016). Other measures under consideration include communication and care coordination activities in partnership with people, their families, and healthcare communities (Marek, Stetzer, Adams, Bub, Schlidt, & Colorafi, 2014). Other measures under consideration include reducing costs and raising efficiency levels by removing the unnecessary duplication of services and appropriate use of services. Finally, safety measures will remain an important part of person- and family-centered approaches by encouraging healthcare systems and providers to include people and their families in decisions and the monitoring of process improvements in the delivery of care. Person-centered approaches, like these, reward value over volume.

Person-Centered Experience Measures

Assessing person-centered care requires specific measurements to help understand a person's disease and illness experience, existing relationships with providers, perceptions of shared power and responsibility, and biopsychosocial characteristics (Hudon, Fortin, Haggerty, Lambert, & Poitras, 2011). Common instruments used to assess person-centered care include a focus on perceptions of hurried communication, partnerships in care, the genuineness of provider–person relationships, health promotion activities, and accumulated knowledge about aspects of care, trust, ongoing care, accessibility, and care utilization (Hudon, Fortin, Haggerty, Lambert, & Poitras, 2011; Koberich & Farin, 2015). These sorts of measures are best captured over time, longitudinally, versus at a specific point in time.

Longitudinal Health Records

Merriam–Webster's Dictionary indicates that longitudinal perspectives involve "the repeated observation or examination of a set of subjects over time" (Merriam, 2017). In similar contexts, a longitudinal health record is defined as "a holistic, dynamic, and integrated plan that documents important disease prevention and treatment goals and plans" (Dykes et al., 2014). In order to satisfy the end objective of developing a longitudinal health record, the EHR has to contain all of a person's pertinent clinical and wellness trending data elements. The data elements cannot be static in a longitudinal health record, reporting only the data elements at a specific moment in time. Partners in care delivery can only anticipate and prevent a possible episodic event using aggregated and dynamic data that provides trends in clinical data elements driven by clinical decision support software. Static clinical data (one data point) will only tell the caregiver that something might be happening at a point in time. It cannot predict an outcome. Of course, projections on limited data do occur but in healthcare this is dangerous as use of limited data can lead to wrong conclusions and possibly errors in decision-making. Components of a longitudinal health record should include items identified in Table 7.1. Adding these components to any health IT development plan will assure greater value for the LTPAC facility.

Table 7.1   Components of a Longitudinal Health Record

- Contains all germane clinical data elements from trusted secure open sources
- Trended over a long period of time including periods of wellness
- Uses analytics and business intelligence software
- Clinical decision support software incorporated
- Person-unique algorithms and the delivery of electronic messages to a person and/or caregiver team
- Continuously updated data
- Enables early intervention to potential incidents
- Assists with medication management
- Assists with therapy/fitness management
- Managed and shared by the person using permissions
- Is secure, private, and HIPAA-compliant
- Based on approved standards
- Basis for a personal health record
- Capable of electronic device
- Used in the transitions of care from one provider to another provider to the person's home of choice

Value Propositions for Technology in LTPAC

Pronouncements by healthcare visionaries conclude the existence of a "new frontier of opportunity for hospitals, health systems, and risk-bearing entities engaged in value-based payments and quality of care improvement programs" (Matheson, Caughey, & Doxey, 2017, p. 14) for those willing to partner with LTPAC provider organizations. Shifts in value-based care are occurring as a result of various external influences such as the Centers for Medicare and Medicaid's efforts to build greater capacity in LTPAC to care for persons caught in the acuity cascade where hospitalized persons are transitioned from higher cost environments (e.g. hospitals) to lower cost settings (LTPAC). One example of this is the Centers for Medicare and Medicaid's Hospital Reductions Program which has funded seven sites across the nation to work with SNFs to reduce hospital readmissions (Ingber et al., 2017). One of the most successful models at reducing hospitalizations is the Missouri Quality Improvement Initiative (MOQI). This model incorporates the use of advanced practice nurses, stressing evidence-based practice, communication, and documentation of advanced care planning decisions made by persons in the SNF and family representatives, as well as the use of technology to securely share personal health information among the care partners (Rantz et al., 2017). In 2016, MOQI reduced hospitalizations of all causes by 33% and potentially avoidable hospitalizations by 48%, the most positive outcome results of the seven national sites in the CMS demonstration. This reduced total Medicare expenses per person by $1,376, saving 33% of the costs of all-cause hospitalizations and 40% of potentially avoidable hospitalizations. Better communication, active engagement, and enhanced partnerships between providers and persons in LTPAC settings and their care representatives were reasons for the success of this model.

With a high-risk person that requires chronic care, such as persons in LTPAC settings, it is quite possible that the hospital rehabilitation post-surgery care plan will not provide the quality of care necessary to prevent an SNF re-hospitalization. Management of acutely ill persons must take into account longitudinal compound effects and interactions of symptoms associated with multiple chronic conditions over time, or greater re-hospitalization rates may occur (Horney, Capp, Boxer, & Burke, 2017). Separate and unique information systems in LTPAC and acute care settings, which contain personal health information, may contribute to breakdowns in communication and the continuity of care during transitions. Healthcare provider's and persons under their care may benefit from a holistic longitudinally focused EHR, called a Longitudinal Electronic Health Record, which takes into account the history of a person and all of their personal health information over the course of a lifetime. This type of electronic record can be facilitated through enhanced health information exchange between care partners, such as hospital staff, LTPAC staff, and the person or family involved in care delivery. This type of exchange requires greater access, trusted partnerships, and a secure electronic infrastructure to facilitate exchange processes.

The Future of LTPAC

Many scenarios exist surrounding the future of the LTPAC sector of care. Some forecast that LTPAC will be absorbed by hospitals and large healthcare systems. It is a difficult time to adapt to the changing of the healthcare system when the current fast-changing regulations and payment system is what LTPAC has to operate under today. An uncertainty of the future drives SNF operators to consider working under numerous payment business models. A skilled nursing facility for example, who traditionally had 95% of its revenue from hospital-discharged Medicare and Medicaid patients, now has to have financial systems to receive payments from bundling and risk payment models from hospitals, alternate care organizations, and managed care financial systems. This, combined with new CMS regulations and low reimbursements, makes it very difficult for LTPAC provider organizations to upgrade their health IT infrastructure. Yet, to survive in this new risk-valued care world, organizations need robust health IT systems.

To be sure, the LTPAC sector cannot keep doing what it has historically been doing. There have been numerous barriers for upgrading an LTPAC health IT infrastructure. Major barriers include:

- Cost of changing to a new health IT vendor
- Cost of the health IT upgrade
- Implementation part-time staff

- ■ Understanding the requirements of the new healthcare system
- ■ Return on investment
- ■ Impact of new or unknown regulations
- ■ Fear of new payment models not covering costs
- ■ Revenue from new payment models not providing revenue to sustain operations

These are valid concerns to a successful future in the new world of person-centered longitudinal care.

Conclusion

This chapter notes that LTPAC can be a highly valued member of person-centered models of care in the U.S. healthcare system. Longitudinal health records are a natural fit for the care delivery system provided for persons in LTPAC settings. However, LTPAC provider organizations must step up and prove quantifiable value within the market. LTPAC health information systems are available to support LTPAC provider organizations in proving their value. The elderly population is growing in number and care complexity as well as cost to Medicare. LTPAC provider organizations, with a person-centered focus, can provide longitudinal care plans in electronic form, which assure a higher quality of life to the elderly population in these settings.

For Discussion

1. Define why each aim under the Quadruple Aim is important for LTPAC leaders to consider.
2. List some examples of how health IT in LTPAC settings helps achieve attributes of person-centered care models.

3. Identify strategies to apply health IT in LTPAC to achieve person-centered care.
4. Express some other values that might be important in differentiating LTPAC from acute and ambulatory care markets.
5. Describe how health IT might facilitate longitudinal care.

References

Abramson, E. L., McGinnis, S., Moore, J., Kaushal, R., & Investigators, H. (2014). A Statewide Assessment of Electronic Health Record Adoption and Health Information Exchange Among Nursing Homes. *Health Services Research,* 49(1 Pt 2), 361–372.

AHRQ. (2016). Agency for Healthcare Research and Quality: Care Coordination. Retrieved from ahrq.gov: https://www.ahrq.gov/professionals/prevention-chronic-care/improve/coordination/index.html website:

Alexander, G. L. (2007). The Nurse-Patient Trajectory Framework. Paper presented at the Medinfo, Brisbane Australia.

Alexander, G. L., Rantz, M., Galambos, C., Vogelsmeier, A., Flesner, M., Popejoy, L. L., ... Elvin, M. (2015). Preparing Nursing Homes for the Future of Health Information Exchange. *Applied Clinical Informatics,* 6(2), 248–266.

Berwick, D. M., Nolan, T. W., & Whittington, J. (2008). The Triple Aim: Care, Health, and Cost. *Health Affairs,* 27(3), 759–769.

Bodenheimer, T., & Sinsky, C. (2014). From Triple to Quadruple Aim: Care of the Patient Requires Care of the Provider. *Annals of Family Medicine,* 12(6), 573–576.

Carman, K. L., Dardess, P., Maurer, M., Sofar, S., Adams, K., Bechtel, C., & Sweeney, J. (2013). Patient and Family Engagement: A Framework for Understanding the Elements and Developing Interventions and Policies. *Health Affairs,* 32(2), 223–231.

Chang, Y. C., Li, J., & Porock, D. (2013). The Effect on Nursing Home Resident Outcomes of Creating a Household Within a Traditional Structure. *Journal of the American Medical Directors Association,* 14(4), 293–299.

Derr, J. (2016). Valued Care Partnership of Post Acute Care. *VBP Monitor.* Retrieved from vpmonitor.com: http://www.vbpmonitor.com/news/item/166-valued-quality-of-care-coordination-vqcc-technology-differential?showall=1 website:

Dykes, P., Samal, L., Donahue, M., Greenberg, J. O., Hurley, A. C., Hasam, O., … Bates, D. W. (2014). A Patient-Centered Longitudinal Care Plan: Vision versus Reality. *Journal of the American Medical Informatics Association,* 21(6), 1082–1090.

Galambos, C., Starr, J., Rantz, M., & Petroski, G. (2016). Analysis of Advanced Directive Documentation to Support Palliative Care Activity in Nursing Homes. *Health and Social Work,* 41(4), 228–234.

Gerteis, M., Edgman-Levitan, S., Daley, J., & Delbanco, T. L. (1993). *Through the Patient's Eyes: Understanding and Promoting Patient-Centered Care.* San Francisco, CA: Josey Bass.

Hetland, B., McAndrew, N., Perazzo, J., & Hickman, R. (2017). A Qualitative Study of Factors that Influence Active Family Involvement with Patient Care in the ICU: Survey of Critical Care Nurses. *Intensive and Critical Care Nursing,* 44, 67–75.

Horney, C., Capp, R., Boxer, R., & Burke, R. E. (2017). Factors Associated with Early Readmission Among Patients Discharged to Post-acute Care Facilities. *Journal of the American Geriatrics Society,* 65(6), 1199–1205.

Hudon, C., Fortin, M., Haggerty, J. L., Lambert, M., & Poitras, M. E. (2011). Measuring Patients' Perceptions of Patient-Centered Care: A Systematic Review of Tools for Family Medicine. *Annals of Family Medicine,* 9(2), 155–164.

Ingber, M. J., Feng, Z., Khatutsky, G., Wang, J.M., Bercaw, L. E., Zheng, N. T., … Segelman, M. (2017). Initiative to Reduce Avoidable Hospitalizations Among Nursing Facility Residents Shows Promising Results. *Health Affairs,* 36(3), 441–450.

IOM. (2001). *Institute of Medicine: Crossing the Quality Chasm: A New Health System for the 21st Century.* Washington, DC: National Academies Press.

Koberich, S., & Farin, E. (2015). A Systematic Review of Instruments Measuring Patients' Perceptions of Patient-Centered Nursing Care. *Nursing Inquiry,* 22(2), 106–120.

Kruse, C. S., Argueta, D. A., Lopez, L., & Nair, A. (2015). Patient and Provider Attitudes Toward the Use of Patient Portals for the Management of Chronic Disease: A Systematic Review. *Journal for Medical Internet Research,* 17(2), e40.

Kruse, C. S., Mileski, M., Alaytsev, V., Carol, E., & Williams, A. (2015). Adoption Factors Associated with Electronic Health Record Among Long-Term Care Facilities: A Systematic Review. *BMJ Open*, 5(1), e006615.

Li, J., & Porock, D. (2014). Resident Outcomes of Person-Centered Care in Long-Term Care: A Narrative Review of Interventional Research. *International Journal of Nursing Studies*, 51(10), 1395–1415.

Lyyra, T. M., & Heikkinen, R. L. (2006). Perceived Social Support and Mortality in Older People. *The Journals of Gerontology, Series B, Psychological Sciences and Social Sciences*, 61, S147–S152.

Marek, K. D., Stetzer, F., Adams, S. J., Bub, D., Schlidt, A., & Colorafi, K. J. (2014). Cost Analysis of a Home-Based Nurse Care Coordination Program. *Journal of the American Geriatrics Society*, 62, 2369–2376.

Matheson, S., Caughey, W., & Doxey, P. (2017). Optimizing the Value of Skilled Nursing Facilities (SNFs) in Value-Based Care: Insights for Hospitals & Health Systems. Retrieved from hubspot.net: https://cdn2.hubspot.net/hubfs/1810303/PDFs/White-Paper-Optimizing-the-Value-of-SNFs-in-Value-Based-Care.pdf:

Merriam–Webster. (2017). Merriam–Webster Online Dictionary. Retrieved from merriam-webster.com: https://www.merriam-webster.com/dictionary/longitudinal.

NQF. (2017). National Quality Forum: Measure Applications Partnership (MAP) 2018 Considerations for Implementing Measures in Federal Programs: MIPS and MSSP (This report is funded by the Department of Health and Human Services under contract HHSM-500-2017-00006I Task Order HHSM-500-T0003). Retrieved from qualityforum.org: http://share.qualityforum.org/Projects/map/Pages/2017-MUC-Comments-Round-2.aspx:

ONC. (2015). Office of the National Coordinator for Health IT: What is a patient portal? Retrieved from healthit.gov: https://www.healthit.gov/providers-professionals/faqs/what-patient-portal

OneView. (2015). OneView Revolutionizing Patient Experience Blog: The Eight Principles of Patient-Centered Care. Retrieved from oneviewhealthcare.com: http://www.oneviewhealthcare.com/the-eight-principles-of-patient-centered-care/ website:

Picker, H. (n.d.). Picker Institute: Picker Principles of Patient Centered Care (12/18). Retrieved from pickerinstitute.org: http://pickerinstitute.org/about/picker-principles/ website:

Popejoy, L. L., Khallilia, M., Popescu, M., Galambos, C., Lyons, V., Rantz, M., ... Stetzer, F. (2015). Quantifying Care Coordination Using Natural Language Processing and Domain-Specific Ontology. *Journal of the Americal Medical Informatics Association*, 22, e93–e103.

Rantz, M., Popejoy, L. L., Vogelsmeier, A., Galambos, C., Alexander, G. L., Flesner, M., ... Petroski, G. F. (2017). Successfully Reducing Hospitalizations of Nursing Home Residents: Results of the Missouri Quality Initiative. *Journal of the American Medical Directors Association*, 18, 960–966.

Reblin, M., & Uchino, B. N. (2008). Social and Emotional Support and Its Implication for Health. *Current Opinions in Psychiatry*, 21(2), 201–205.

Rogers, C. R. (1980). *Foundations of a Person-Centered Approach: A Way of Being*. Boston, MA: Houghton Mifflin.

Stoicea, N., You, T., Eiterman, A., Hartwell, C., Davila, V., Marjoribanks, S., ... Rogers, B. (2017). Perspectives of Post-Acute Transition of Care for Cardiac Surgery Patients. *Frontiers in Cardiac Medicine*, 4, 70.

Suchman, A. L. (1994). Book Review: Through the Patient's Eyes: Understanding and Promoting Patient-Centered Care. *New England Journal of Medicine*, 330, 873.

Winland-Brown, J., Lachman, V. D., & O'Connor Swanson, E. (2015). The New 'Code of Ethics for Nurses With Interpretive Statements' (2015): Practical Clinical Application, Part I. *MedSurg*, 24(4), 268–271.

Yeaman, B., Ko, K. J., & del Castillo, R. A. (2015). Care Transitions in Long-term Care and Acute Care: Health Information Exchange and Readmission Rate. *Online Journal of Issues in Nursing*, September 30, 20(3), 5.

Chapter 8

International Perspectives on LTPAC HIT

Learning Objectives

Reading this chapter will help you to

- Describe international landscapes for health IT in LTPAC.
- List IT capabilities found by international region.
- Express measurable outcomes by IT capabilities among multiple regions of the world.

Introduction

The world's population is aging. Every developed country in the world is experiencing growth in the number and proportion of older persons in their population. Arguably, a success story in the history of humankind, population aging is poised to become one of the most significant forces transforming societies in the twenty-first century. Indeed, the days of setting elderly members of society aside are over. Individuals want to live a meaningful life throughout their entire lifespans, with some giving priority to "quality of life" over "quality of care."

> If you have a healthcare incident you need quality of care to bring you back to the best quality of life possible.
>
> *(Derr at the LTPAC Health IT 2014 Summit.)*

The implications of an aging population are apparent in nearly all sectors of society, to include health IT. In response, leaders throughout the industrialized world are taking steps to learn from each other about how to address the challenges (and opportunities) of an aging populace. Notwithstanding cultural variances regarding the role and position the elderly play in different societies, the synergies resulting from these efforts can be very positive for all involved.

Recognizing the value of looking outside the confines of one's cultural milieu, it is most fitting to close this textbook with a brief survey of LTPAC health IT approaches in select countries outside of the United States. Though in no ways an exhaustive review of countries and health IT efforts, the following is intended to encourage the LTPAC health IT professional to think beyond the confines of their local environment.

International Commonwealth Fund

The International Commonwealth Fund, a not-for-profit organization whose mission is to promote a high-performing healthcare system that achieves better access, improved quality, and greater efficiency, identified ten challenges high-performing healthcare systems around the world need to address. Targeted towards systems caring for older, frail adults with advancing illness and complex conditions, several of the recommendations have direct application to LTPAC stakeholders

(The Commonwealth Fund International Experts Working Group on Patients with Complex Needs, 2017).

1. Make care coordination a high priority.
2. Identify patients in greatest need of proactive, coordinated care.
3. Train more primary care physicians and geriatricians.
4. Facilitate communication between providers (e.g. clinical record integration).
5. Engage patients in decisions about their care.
6. Provide better support for caregivers.
7. Redesign funding mechanisms to meet patients' needs.
8. Integrate health and social services, and physical and mental healthcare.
9. Engage clinicians in change and train and support clinical leaders.
10. Learn from experience and scale up successful projects.

The recommendations are significant for the present purposes as it provides a framework for exploring international LTPAC HIT initiatives designed to support these recommendations.

Surveying International Landscapes

The growing technology revolution in aged care is not limited to certain geographical areas. The revolution is taking place worldwide. A recent literature review about long-term care and technology conducted from 2000 to 2017 identified 87 articles (Alexander et al., unpublished maunscript). In this review, just over 55% of the articles include relevant studies from the United States, nearly 12% from Belgium, Hong Kong, Singapore, Spain, and Taiwan, 11% include studies from Australia, 10% from Germany, Norway, and Sweden, and nearly 9% represent the countries Portugal, Canada, England, France, New Zealand, Scotland, Serbia, and Switzerland.

Technologies and associated outcomes are listed among the geographical regions in two periods: 2000–2010 (Table 8.1) and 2011–2017 (Table 8.2).

Select examples by geographical region, from the articles cited in Tables 8.1 and 8.2, providing evidential support of the International Commonwealth Fund's recommendations, follow.

North America

Through nearly the first 17 years of the twenty-first century, the United States and Canada appear to have explored the use of health information technology in long-term care settings more than any other country. That said, there was no evidence of LTPAC health IT research in Mexico or Central America.

During the 2000–2010 period, the most common types of technologies studied involved the implementation of electronic health/medical records to support nursing care (Alexander, Rantz, Flesner, Diekemper, & Siem, 2007). Researchers also appeared to be interested in describing outcomes for initial IT implementation strategies, as well as informing administrators about barriers and facilitators to IT adoption (Brandeis, Hogan, Murphy, & Murray, 2007; Cherry, Carter, Owen, & Lockhart, 2008; Rantz et al., 2010; Vogelsmeier, Halbesleben, & Scott-Cawiezell, 2008). These studies are important as they functioned to inform the LTPAC community how to strategize their own adoption methods, especially those organizations without IT personnel embedded in their own facilities to guide implementations. Other North American research assessments of electronic clinical tools during this period focused on specific forms of technology, such as clinical decision support systems (CDSS). One study, for example, found that some CDSS used in pharmacy IT systems provides important reminders to clinicians about adverse drugs that might lead to adverse reactions (Handler et al., 2008). These reminders act as early notifications to providers of potential clinical problems enabling them to

Table 8.1 Technologies and Associated Outcomes Listed Geographically from 2000 to 2010

Country	Technology	Outcomes
France	Electronic e-mail with monitoring system	Implementation issues
Germany	Information and communication technology in aged care	Ethical assumptions of personal responsibility
Norway	Electronic patient record	Perceptions of electronic patient records
Singapore	Web browsing technology and broadband communication	Teleconsultation
Spain	Web-based tele-dermatology system	Dermatologist referral and documentation
	Smart wearable devices and mobile technology	Describe system prototype of microchips installed in clothing apparel of patients
Sweden	Passage alarms, sensor-activated nighttime illumination, fall detectors, internet	Job satisfaction and perceived quality of care
Taiwan	Telemedicine/Telehealth	Perceptions and expectations of telemedicine
		Hospital readmission rates, medication non-adherence, adverse drug events

(Continued)

**Table 8.1 (Continued)   Technologies and Associated Outcomes
Listed Geographically from 2000 to 2010**

Country	Technology	Outcomes
USA	Web-based research information system	Health-related quality of life measures
	Telemedicine	Communication between and among health professionals
	Computerized physician order entry (CPOE)	Medication prescribing and medication error
	Pharmaceutical care planning software	Use of information technology by pharmacists
	CPOE, clinical decision support	Medication errors and preventable drug-related injuries
	Electronic health/medical records	Initial implementation strategies
		Barriers and facilitators to adoption
		Cost, staffing, and quality impact
		Staff efficiencies, quality indicators, information exchange
	After-hours telephone calls (TrAC)	Key characteristics of after-hour calls
	Web-based error reporting system	Medication errors and preventable drug-related injuries
	Clinical decision support system in EHR	Relationship between frequency of alerts and triggers and quality measures

(*Continued*)

Table 8.1 (Continued)   Technologies and Associated Outcomes Listed Geographically from 2000 to 2010

Country	Technology	Outcomes
		Describe alerts and associated triggers used in nursing home IT
	Clinical event monitoring system	Detection of adverse drug reactions in NH
	Electronic medication administration records	Types of medication errors
		Implementation and workarounds
	Assessing IT infrastructure	Identify diversity of IT being implemented and survey development
	Laboratory health information technology	Usage of laboratory health information technology in nursing home
	Web-based resource for self-management and messaging services	Quality of life in CHF patients
	Standardized nurse's aide documentation	Pressure ulcer prevention in long-term care facilities (nursing homes)

change a course of action, reduce the risk of injury, and enhance patient safety. Similarly, the importance of electronic medication administration records and their use in LTPAC settings was evident as investigators explored implementation strategies, workarounds, and the epidemiology of medication errors (Pierson et al., 2007; Rochon et al., 2005; Scott-Cawiezell et al. 2009). Other emerging forms of technology studied include web-based platforms to perform specific functions such as reporting health-related quality of life measures, error reporting systems, and providing electronic

Table 8.2   Technologies and Associated Outcomes Listed Geographically from 2011 to 2017

Country	Technology	Outcomes
Australia	Electronic nursing documentation system	Documentation of activities
		Proportions of time spent on caregivers' time after IT implementation
		Efficiency of documentation by caregivers
	Electronic health records in residential aged care	Three categories of benefits have been realized to staff members, residents and residential aged care facilities (RACFs)
		Unintended consequences of implementation
	Health information exchange	Identify key work processes in health information exchange
	Storage of medication information	Discover how medication information is translated across aged care settings
	Information and communication technology (ICT) in aged care	Identify issues that affect adoption of ICT in aged care
	Electronic nursing care plans	Documentation audit of electronic nursing care plans in aged care facilities

(Continued)

Table 8.2 (Continued) Technologies and Associated Outcomes Listed Geographically from 2011 to 2017

Country	Technology	Outcomes
Belgium	Clinical decision support system for pressure ulcer prevention	Adherence to pressure ulcer prevention guidelines
	Semantic cloud-based system for context-aware services	Scalability- and performance-based study
Canada	Use of personal digital assistants and tablets for assessing evidence-based information	Impact of technology on nurses' use patterns
England	Telehealth and telecare	Participants' perspectives on design features
Germany	Computer-based nursing records	Staff experiences with implementation
	Short message service and voice call interventions	Adherence to medical advice
Hong Kong	Implementation of clinical information systems in nursing homes	Critical barriers to implementation
Netherlands	Computer system to support medication reviews	Planned approach for evaluating clinical rules in a medication review IT system
	InterRAI long-term care facility assessment software with decision support	Facilitating and impeding factors during initial and maintenance phases
	Surveillance technology to monitor residents	Exploring benefits and drawbacks of technology

(Continued)

Table 8.2 (Continued)   Technologies and Associated Outcomes Listed Geographically from 2011 to 2017

Country	Technology	Outcomes
	Electronic technologies supporting aging in place	Overview of factors influencing technology acceptance
	26 different types of technology	Technology acceptance
New Zealand	Home-based remote monitoring technology	Quality of life in CHF and COPD patients at home
Norway	Computer decision support for pressure ulcers and malnutrition care planning	Completeness and comprehensiveness of documentation of pressure ulcers and malnutrition
	Global Position System (GPS)	Autonomy and independence of persons in the community
Portugal	Telehealth care	Innovations in roaming monitoring systems, home monitoring systems, central care service monitoring systems
Scotland	An overview of various assisted living technologies	Proposed model for functional assistive living technology research and development
Serbia	Horizontal integration between LTC and hospitals' data sharing, coordination, and communication pathways	Proposed model for future internet assembly

(Continued)

Table 8.2 (Continued) Technologies and Associated Outcomes Listed Geographically from 2011 to 2017

Country	Technology	Outcomes
Spain	A variety of home technologies used in the kitchen	Usability and physical, sensory, and cognitive accessibility
Sweden	Services that assist elderly in the procurement, preparation, and social construct of eating food	User requirements, technical feasibility, and implementation of system using 13 potential e-services
	Database-centric architecture for smart homes and ambient assisted living	Bed exits and common room transitions and deviations during the night
Switzerland	Sensors, medical images, and signal processing	Systematic review of field of medical sensors, signals, and imaging informatics
USA	Sensor technology interface	Interface improvements designed for residents, caregivers, clinicians
	Industry standards for health information technology use in pharmacy	Annual survey describing implementation of pharmacy technology solutions
	Geriatric Risk Assessment MedGuide (GRAM) informatics tool	Automated monitoring plans for falls and delirium
	Electronic health/medical records	Facilitators and barriers to adoption
		Baseline assessments of electronic health record adoption

(Continued)

**Table 8.2 (Continued) Technologies and Associated Outcomes
Listed Geographically from 2011 to 2017**

Country	Technology	Outcomes
		Development of an IT readiness assessment tool
		Differences in level of health IT adoption in nursing homes
		Clinical care quality indicators, resident awareness, and satisfaction with IT
		Staff perceptions, implementation challenges, and barriers
	Implementation of infection control programs and IT	Infrastructure of infection control IT
	Automated drug dispensing systems	A brief including an introduction to automated dispensing systems
	Clinical decision support	Clinical decision support tools to prevent pressure ulcers
		Reduction of in-house acquired pressure ulcer incidence rates
	Electronic patient falls reporting system	Stakeholders' perspectives, system-level benefits costs, usability, users' physical, cognitive, and macro-ergonomic challenges

(Continued)

Table 8.2 (Continued) Technologies and Associated Outcomes Listed Geographically from 2011 to 2017

Country	Technology	Outcomes
	Computer-generated rounding reports	Physician workflow
	E-prescribing	Brief on regulations and growing use of technology by pharmacists
	Smart phones and remote monitoring devices	Implementation challenges and access to technology
	Information and communication technology (ICT)	Interactions between providers using social network analysis in facilities with varied levels of IT
	Touch screen technology delivering psychosocial nondrug interventions	Usability measures, engagement, simplification of daily living
	Sensor systems	Length of stay and costs of care delivery
	Health Information Exchange (HIE)	Inpatient readmission and return emergency department visits
		Developing use cases for HIE implementation in nursing homes
		HIE implementation
		Assessing baseline levels of EHR and HIE adoption in nursing homes

resources for self-management and messaging services for chronically ill patients (Bowles, Peng, Qian, & Naylor, 2001; Brennan et al., 2010).

During the 2011–2017 period, most of the research on electronic health/medical records took place in the latter part of the decade. A myriad of reasons may have influenced the growth in this type of research to include the increase in IT adoption by LTPAC provider organizations. This period also witnessed the increased availability of innovative informatics tools drawing the interest of researchers. For example, sensor technology interfaces used as early warning systems for condition changes began to surface, supporting the electronic visualization of mobility and functional status data from LTPAC residents living independently in the community (Alexander et al., 2011). These types of resources enable the early detection of decline in mobility and functional status in LTPAC residents, allowing the care team to intervene and avoid unwanted events like hospitalizations. Another advance during this time was the incorporation of health information exchanges to provide secure connections between internal nursing facility staff and external entities, such as hospital personnel or clinical laboratories (Abramson, McGinnis, Moore, Kaushal, & HITEC investigators, 2014). These health information exchanges provide secure electronic channels to pass clinical information between clinical settings in order to enable the seamless transmission of personal health information, such as discharge summaries or medication reconciliation documentation (Alexander et al., 2015; Yeaman, Ko, & Alvarez del Castillo, 2015).

Australia

Research about health IT in LTPAC settings in this region of the world occurred primarily after 2010. These studies tended to investigate the benefits of implementing health IT as realized by staff, residents, and resident-aged care facilities as a whole (Munyisia, Yu, & Hailey, 2012; Zhang, Yu, & Shen, 2012). In other studies, authors attempted to identify and characterize the unintended consequences of implementing health IT (Yu, Zhang, Gong, & Zhang, 2013). For instance, a poor fit between an electronic health record and an IT clinical laboratory reporting system was associated with data loss, reduced decision time, and unnecessary testing, resulting in negative outcomes like increased hospitalizations or greater cost due to repeated testing. Anticipating and recognizing unintended consequences of health IT can reduce or even alleviate these negative occurrences. Similar experiments attempting to characterize the unintended consequences of health IT have occurred in other countries.

Other Australian studies about health IT in LTPAC settings have focused on gaining efficiencies for clinical staff by assessing the amount of time clinicians spend using health IT systems to document care (Munyisia, Yu, & Hailey, 2012). Greater efficiencies may translate into more time for a clinician to spend at the bedside, increased time for clinician–patient interaction, and perhaps earlier recognition of a condition change and subsequent intervention.

The efficient and secure transmission of health information using technology was an important development in some Australian studies. For example, one study focused on detailing the dynamic workflows occurring between caregivers during health information exchanges (Georgiou, Marks, Braithwaite, & Westbrook, 2013). The availability of this information was found to inspire caregiver confidence and functioned to support strategic initiatives by other area LTPAC leaders.

Asia

Prior to 2010, the earliest research developments in Asia focused on the use of web browsing technology and broadband communication to conduct remote teleconsultations

(P.M.D.S. & KC, 2001). More specifically, telehealth and telemedicine systems supported the care delivery of LTPAC residents in Singapore and Taiwan (Chang, Chen, & Chang, 2009). Initial studies in this region explored caregiver and patient perceptions of telehealth and telemedicine approaches. Other studies explored definitive organizational outcomes such as the impact of telemedicine on hospital readmission rates, adherence to medications, and adverse events (Hsu & Sandford, 2007). After 2010, studies about the facilitators and barriers to clinical information system implementation began to appear in Asia (Or, Dohan, & Tan, 2014).

Europe

At the start of this century, researchers in European countries (France and Germany) were evaluating the implementation and ethical issues of information and communication technology use in LTPAC settings, to include the transmission of information through electronic e-mail systems (Noury et al., 2006; Remmers, 2010). There were early innovators in Sweden as well, experimenting with internet modalities supporting sensor alarms designed to detect movement, active illumination, and patient falls (Engstrom, Ljunggren, Lindqvist, & Carlsson, 2005). These innovators were particularly interested in user satisfaction and perceptions of how these devices affected quality of care.

After 2010, European LTPAC technology evaluations increased. Studies included design features for telecare and telehealth systems in LTPAC settings (Rocha, 2011), the implementation of electronic computer-based records and associated capabilities, as well as the impact these systems had on quality (e.g. adherence to evidence-based guidelines and medical advice) (Norway and Belgium) (Beeckman et al., 2013; Fossum, Alexander, Ehnfors, & Ehrenberg, 2011; Fossum, Ehnfors, Svensson, Hansen, & Ehrenberg, 2013). Additional capabilities of interest during this time included computerized systems with automated clinical rules to support medication reviews, assessment software with decision rules to better identify risk, and technology to support independent community living environments to help older people age in place (Netherlands, Scotland, and Sweden) (Boorsma, Langedijk, Frijters, & van Hout, 2013; de Wit HA, 2013). Investigators also began developing horizontally integrated systems by creating connections between hospitals and LTPAC environments to promote data sharing, improve care coordination, and secure communication pathways (Urošević & Mitić, 2014).

Conclusion

Researchers and innovators in LTPAC settings around the world are well on their way towards meeting international recommendations to use technology to assist in improving processes of care (e.g. identifying the most vulnerable at-risk patients, implementing care coordination models to reduce fragmentation, and lowering the risk for poor outcomes). One fact remains clear from this international review; *LTPAC provider organizations across the world leverage similar technologies to address congruous patient care problems.* LTPAC leaders, interested in improving care delivery for elderly residents, can learn much by promoting collaborations with others whether the collaborations be with those in neighboring communities or distant countries.

For Discussion

1. Identify the regions of the world where research surrounding the adoption of health IT in LTPAC settings is most prevalent.
2. Discuss the pros and cons of using insights gained from health IT research from countries outside the United States.

References

Abramson, E. L., McGinnis, S., Moore, J., Kaushal, R., & HITEC investigators. (2014). A Statewide Assessment of Electronic Health Record Adoption and Health Information Exchange Among Nursing Homes. *Health Services Research*, 49(1 Pt 2), 361–372.

Alexander, G. L., Rantz, M., Flesner, M., Diekemper, M., & Siem C. (2007). Clinical Information Systems in Nursing Homes: An Evaluation of Initial Implementation Strategies. *Computers Informatics Nursing*, 25(4), 189–197.

Alexander, G. L., Rantz, M., Skubic, M., Koopman, R. J., Phillips, L. J., Guevara, R. D., & Miller, S. J. (2011). Evolution of an Early Illness Warning System to Monitor Frail Elders in Independent Living. *Journal of Healthcare Engineering*, 2(2), 259–286.

Alexander, G. L., Rantz, M., Galambos, C., Vogelsmeier, A., Flesner, M., Popejoy, L., Mueller, J., Shumate, S., & Elvin, M. (2015). Preparing Nursing Homes for the Future of Health Information Exchange. *Applied Clinical Informatics*, 6(2), 248–266.

Alexander G. L., A., Doughty, K., Hornblow, A., Livingstone, A., Dougherty, M., Jacobs, S., & Fisk, M. (unpublished manuscript). *Advancing Aged Care Roadmaps with Health IT in Long Term Care.*

Beeckman, D., Clays, E., Van Hecke, A., Vanderwee, K., Schoonhoven, L., & Verhaeghe, S. (2013). A Multi-faceted Tailored Strategy to Implement an Electronic Clinical Decision Support System for Pressure Ulcer Prevention in Nursing Homes: A Two-armed Randomized Controlled Trial. *International Journal of Nursing Studies*, 50(4), 475–486.

Boorsma, M., Langedijk, E., Frijters, D., & van Hout, H. P. J. (2013). Implementation of Geriatric Assessment and Decision Support in Residential Care Homes: Facilitating and Impeding Factors During Initial and Maintenance Phase. *BMC Health Services Research*, 13(8), 1–9.

Bowles, K., Peng, T., Qian, R., & Naylor, M. (2001). Informatics application provides instant research to practice benefits. *Proceedings American Medical Informatics Association*, 66–77.

Brandeis, G. H., Hogan, M., Murphy, M., & Murray, S. (2007). Electronic Health Record Implementation in Community Nursing Homes. *Journal of the American Medical Directors Association*, 8, 31–34.

Brennan, P. F., Casper, G. R., Burke, L. J., Johnson, K. A., Brown, R., Valdez, R. S., ... Sturgeon, B. (2010). Technology-Enhanced Practice for Patients with Chronic Cardiac Disease: Home Implementation and Evaluation. *Heart and Lung*, 39(6), S34–S46.

Chang, J. Y., Chen, L. K., & Chang, C. C. (2009). Perspectives and Expectations for Telemedicine Opportunities from Families of Nursing Home Residents and Caregivers in Nursing Homes. *International Journal of Medical Informatics*, 78(7), 494–502.

Cherry, B., Carter, M., Owen, D., & Lockhart C. (2008). Factors Affecting Electronic Health Record Adoption in Long-Term Care Facilities. *Journal of Healthcare Quality*, 30(2), 37–47.

de Wit, H. A., Mestres Gonzalvo, C., Hurkens, K. P., Mulder, W. J., Janknegt, R., Verhey, F. R., ... van der Kuy, P. H. (2013). Development of a Computer System to Support Medication Reviews in Nursing Homes. *International Journal of Clinical Pharmacy*, 35(5), 668–672.

Engström, M., Ljunggren, B., Lindqvist, R., & Carlsson, M. (2005). Staff Perceptions of Job Satisfaction and Life Situation Before and 6 and 12 Months After Increased Information Technology Support in Dementia Care. *Journal of Telemedicine & Telecare*, 11(6), 304–309.

Fossum, M., Alexander, G. L., Ehnfors, M., & Ehrenberg, A. (2011). Effects of a Computerized Decision Support System on Pressure Ulcers and Malnutrition in Nursing Homes for the Elderly. *International Journal of Medical Informatics*, September, 80(9), 607–617.

Fossum, M., Ehnfors, M., Svensson, E., Hansen, L. M., & Ehrenberg, A. (2013). Effects of a Computerized Decision Support System on Care Planning for Pressure Ulcers and Malnutrition in Nursing Homes: An Intervention Study. *International Journal of Medical Informatics*, 82(10), 911–921.

Georgiou, A., Marks, A., Braithwaite, J., & Westbrook, J. I. (2013). Gaps, Disconnections, and Discontinuities-The Role of Information Exchange in the Delivery of Quality Long-Term Care. *The Gerontologist*, 53(5), 770–779.

Handler, S. H., Hanlon, J. T., Perera, S., Saul, M., Fridsma, D., Visweswaran, S., Studenski, S., ... Becich, M. e. (2008). Assessing the performance characteristics of signals used by a clinical event monitor to detect adverse drug reactions in the nursing home. *American Medical Informatics Conference.* Washington DC.

Hsu, C.-C., & Sandford B. A. (2007). The Delphi Technique: Making Sense of Consensus. *Practical Assessment, Research & Evaluation,* 12(10), 1–8.

Munyisia, E. N., Yu, P., & Hailey, D. (2012). The Impact of an Electronic Nursing Documentation System on Efficiency of Documentation by Caregivers in a Residential Aged Care Facility. *Journal of Clinical Nursing,* 21, 2940–2948.

Noury, N., Villemazet, C., Fleury, A., Barralon, P., Rumeau, P., Vuillerme, N., Baghai, R., & editor. (2006). Ambient Multi-Perceptive System with Electronic Mails for a Residential Health Monitoring System. *Engineering in Biology and Medicine.* New York: IEEE.

Or, C., Dohan, M., & Tan, J. (2014). Understanding Critical Barriers to Implementing a Clinical Information System in a Nursing Home through the Lens of a Socio-technical Perspective. *Journal of Medical Systems,* September, 38(9), 99.

P.M.D.S., P., & KC, L. (2001). EMR based tele-geriatric system. Studies in Health Technology & Informatics. *Proceedings of MedInfo,* 849–853.

Pierson, S., Hansen, R., Green, S., Williams, C., Akers, R., Jonsson, M., & Carey, T. (2007). Preventing Medication Errors in Long-term Care: Results and Evaluation of a Large-Scale Web-Based Error Reporting System. *Quality & Safety in Health Care,* 16(4), 297–302.

Rantz, M. J., Hicks, L., Petroski, G. F., Madsen, R. W., Alexander, G., Galambos, C., … Greenwald, L. (2010). Cost, Staffing and Quality Impact of Bedside Electronic Medical Record (EMR) in Nursing Homes. *Journal of the American Medical Directors Association,* 11(7), 485–493.

Remmers, H. (2010). Environments for Ageing, Assistive Technology and Self-Determination: Ethical Perspectives. *Informatics for Health & Social Care,* 35(3–4), 200–210.

Rochon, P. A., Field, T. S., Bates, D. W., Lee, M., Gavendo, L., Erramuspe-Mainard, J., … Gurwitz, J. H. (2005). Computerized Physician Order Entry with Clinical Decision Support in the Long-Term Care Setting: Insights from the Baycrest Centre for Geriatric Care. *Journal of the American Geriatrics Society,* 53(10), 1780–1789.

Rocha, Álvaro. (2011). Evolution of Information Systems and Technologies Maturity in Healthcare. *International Journal of Healthcare Information Systems and Informatics*, 6(2), 28–36.

Scott-Cawiezell, J., Madsen, R. W., Pepper, G. A., Vogelsmeier, A., Petroski, G., & Zellmer, D. (2009). Medication Safety Teams' Guided Implementation of Electronic Medication Administration Records in Five Nursing Homes. *Joint Commission Journal on Quality and Patient Safety*, 35(1), 29–35.

The Commonwealth Fund International Experts Working Group on Patients with Complex Needs. (2017). *Designing a High-Performing Health Care System for Patients with Complex Needs, Expanded and Revised Edition.* The Commonwealth Fund.

Uroševic, V., & Mitic, M. (2014). From Generic Pathways to ICT-supported Horizontally Integrated Care: The SmartCare Approach and Convergence with Future Internet Assembly. *Studies in Health Technology & Informatics: Cross-Border Challenges in Informatics with a Focus on Disease Surveillance and Utilising Big-Data*, 197, 71–75.

Vogelsmeier, A. A., Halbesleben, J. R. B., & Scott-Cawiezell, J. R. (2008). Technology Implementation and Workarounds in the Nursing Home. *Journal of the American Medical Informatics Association*, 15, 114–119.

Yeaman, B., Ko, K. J., & Alvarez del Castillo, R. (2015). Care Transitions in Long-term Care and Acute Care: Health Information Exchange and Readmission Rate. *Online Journal of Issues in Nursing*, September 30, 20(3), 5.

Yu, P., Zhang, Y., Gong, Y., & Zhang, J. (2013). Unintended Adverse Consequences of Introducing Electronic Health Records in Residential Aged Care Homes. *International Journal of Medical Informatics*, 82, 772–788.

Zhang, Y., Yu, P., & Shen, J. (2012). The Benefits of Introducing Electronic Health Records in Residential Aged Care Facilities: A Multiple Case Study. *International Journal of Medical Informatics*, 81, 690–704.

Index

2018 proposed revised payment system, 20
21st Century Cures Act of 2016, 20

Academic medical centers (AMCs), 11
Acceptance testing, 91
Accountable care organizations (ACOs), 15
Accounts payable (AP), 36
Accounts receivable (AR), 123
ACOs, *see* Accountable care organizations (ACOs)
Activities of daily living (ADL), 18, 149
Administrative applications, 34–35
Administrative safeguards, 106
Adoption of solution, 86
Agency for Healthcare Research and Quality (AHRQ), 21, 40, 47
ALF, *see* Assisted living facilities (ALF)
Alternative payment models (APMs), xviii–xx, xxi, 15–16
AMCs, *see* Academic medical centers (AMCs)
American Nurse Association, 152
American Recovery and Reinvestment Act (ARRA), 19

Ancillary medical services, 15
AP, *see* Accounts payable (AP)
APMs, *see* Alternative payment models (APMs)
Applications, in healthcare IT, 34–44
  administrative, 34–35
  clinical, 36–41
  financial, 35–36
  standardized data elements, 43–44
  standards and interoperability, 41–43
Appraisal process, 137–138
AR, *see* Accounts receivable (AR)
ARRA, *see* American Recovery and Reinvestment Act (ARRA)
Asia, 183–184
Assisted living facilities (ALF), xv, 45
Attestation, 107
Australia, 182–183
Authentication, 107
Authorization, 107
Automated testing, 89–90

Balanced Budget Act of 1997 (BBA), 18
Big bang approach, 86–87
Billing and accounting, 45, 46

Black-box testing, 90
BPR, *see* Business process
      reengineering (BPR)
Broadband communication, 183
Budgets, 122
Build *vs.* Buy decision, 73–78
Business continuity plan, 98
Business ethics, 124
Business intelligence management, 69
Business operations, 122–123
Business process reengineering
      (BPR), 68
Business requirements, 65–71

CAHIMS, *see* Certified Association
      in Healthcare Information
      and Management Systems
      (CAHIMS)
Call-abandonment rate, 140
Carolinas HealthCare System
      (CHS), 6
Cause-and-effect relationships, 61
CCD, *see* Continuity of Care
      Document (CCD)
C-CDA, *see* Composite Clinical
      Document Architecture
      (C-CDA)
CCRC, *see* Continuing care
      retirement communities
      (CCRC)
CDS, *see* Clinical Decision
      Support (CDS)
CDSS, *see* Clinical decision support
      systems (CDSS)
Center for Clinical Standards and
      Quality, 109
Centers for Medicare and Medicaid
      Services (CMS), 21, 161
CEO, *see* Chief executive officer (CEO)
Certified Professional in
      Healthcare Information
      and Management Systems
      (CPHIMS), xxviii, 136

CFO, *see* Chief financial officer (CFO)
Change control, 91
Change management, 67, 86, 87–88
Chief executive officer (CEO),
      59, 132
Chief financial officer (CFO), 59
Chief information officer (CIO),
      59, 132
Chief information security officer
      (CISO), 104, 132
Chief medical information officer
      (CMIO), 132
Chief nursing information officer
      (CNIO), 132
Chief technology officer (CTO), 132
Children's Health Insurance
      Program (CHIP), 21
Children's hospitals, 11
CHIP, *see* Children's Health
      Insurance Program (CHIP)
Chronic care comorbidity care,
      149–150
CHS, *see* Carolinas HealthCare
      System (CHS)
CIA, *see* Confidentiality, Integrity,
      and Availability (CIA) triad
CIO, *see* Chief information
      officer (CIO)
CISO, *see* Chief information security
      officer (CISO)
Clients, 31
Client terminals, 32–33
Clinical applications, 36–41
Clinical charting, 44
Clinical Decision Support (CDS), 41
Clinical decision support systems
      (CDSS), 172
Clinical technology
    current-state analysis, 70–71
    future-state analysis, 71
    prioritizing, 71
    stakeholder sign-off, 71
Clinician/practitioner consultant, 134

Cloud computing, 31
CMIO, *see* Chief medical
    information officer (CMIO)
CMS, *see* Centers for Medicare and
    Medicaid Services (CMS)
CNIO, *see* Chief nursing information
    officer (CNIO)
Code of Ethics, 152
Communication, 119–120, 130
    plan, 96
    preparation, 119–120
    presentation, 120
Compliance/risk management
    leader, 104–105
Composite Clinical Document
    Architecture (C-CDA), 16, 20
Confidentiality, Integrity, and
    Availability (CIA) triad,
    102–103
Continuing care retirement
    communities (CCRC),
    xv–xxii
Continuity of Care Document
    (CCD), 16, 20
CPHIMS, *see* Certified Professional
    in Healthcare Information
    and Management Systems
    (CPHIMS)
Critical access hospitals (CAH), 11
CRM, *see* Customer relationship
    management (CRM)
CTO, *see* Chief technology
    officer (CTO)
Customer relationship management
    (CRM), 46
Customers, 139
Customer support, 97
Cybersecurity, 109

DAMA, *see* Data Management
    International (DAMA)
Data, 30
Data architecture management, 69

Data backup plan, 109
Database operations management, 69
Data conversion, 67
Data development, 69
Data flows, 96
Data governance, 69, 104–105
Data integration, 33, 103
Data management, 69–70, 105–107
Data Management International
    (DAMA), 68
Data quality management, 69
Data security, 69, 101–102
Data storage, 33
Data warehousing, 69
Define, measure, analyze, improve,
    and control (DMAIC), 61
Department documentation,
    127–128
DeSalvo, Karen, 148
Devices, data integration from, 93–94
Diagnosis-Related Groups (DRGs),
    xvi, xvii
Digital Imaging and
    Communications in
    Medicine (DICOM), 43
Disaster recovery, 66–67
    and business continuity plan,
    108–109
    plan, 98
    procedures, 109
Discharged not final billed
    (DNFB), 123
Disciplinary action, 138
Disrupted healthcare information
    systems (HIS) operations,
    97–98
DMAIC, *see* Define, measure,
    analyze, improve, and
    control (DMAIC)
DNFB, *see* Discharged not final
    billed (DNFB)
Document and content
    management, 69

Downtime plan, 98
Downtime procedures, 96
DRGs, *see* Diagnosis-Related
    Groups (DRGs)
Due diligence, 76–78

eAssessments, 149
EHR, *see* Electronic health
    record (EHR)
The Eight Picker Principals of
    Patient-Centered Care,
    152–158
  access to care, 158
  care coordination and integration
    of services, 153–154
  continuity and transition,
    157–158
  emotional support, 155–156
  family and friends, 156
  information and education, 154
  physical comfort, 154–155
  respecting and treating persons,
    152–153
Einstein, Albert, 59
Electronic computer-based
    records, 184
Electronic e-mail systems, 184
Electronic health record (EHR),
    xxvii, 7, 40, 101, 133–134
Electronic medical records
    (EMR), 40
Electronic medication
    administration records
    (eMAR), 44, 175
Electronic remittance notice
    (ERN), 46
Electronic treatment administration
    records (eTAR), 44
eMAR, *see* Electronic medication
    administration records
    (eMAR)
Emergency-mode operation
    plan, 109

Employee development, 134–138
  healthcare IT certifications, 136
  IT-based certifications, 135
  professional, 136–137
  training and in-service
    programs, 135
EMR, *see* Electronic medical
    records (EMR)
EMR Adoption Model (EMRAM), 47
EO, *see* Executive Order (EO)
ERN, *see* Electronic remittance
    notice (ERN)
eTAR, *see* Electronic treatment
    administration records (eTAR)
Europe, 184–185
Executive Order (EO), 19

Family caregivers, 10
FDA, *see* Food and Drug
    Administration (FDA)
Fee-for-service (FFS), xix, xvi, xvii,
    xviii, 9, 15, 60
Financial applications, 35–36
Financial benchmarks, 122–123
First-call resolution rate, 140
Five Whys, 61
Food and Drug Administration
    (FDA), 22

Gap analysis, 125–126
General ledger, 35
General medical hospitals, 11
Goals and organization, 118
Government-financed and managed
    insurance programs, 8
Government regulations, 68
Gray-box testing, 90

Hands-on training, 94
HCBS, *see* Home- and community-
    based services (HCBS)
Health and Human Services (HHS),
    19, 21, 148

Healthcare environment, and
LTPAC, 3–23
alternative payment models
(APMs), 15–16
ancillary medical services, 15
delivery of healthcare services,
16–22
laws and regulations, 17–20
regulatory bodies, 20–22
healthcare provider
organizations, 10–14
healthcare providers, 9–10
overview, 3–4
patients/consumers, 5–7
payers, 8–9
Healthcare Financial Management
Association (HFMA), 35
Healthcare IT certifications, 136
Healthcare provider organizations,
10–14
community health, 12
hospitals, 11–12
location, 11–12
ownership type, 11
service type, 11
teaching status, 11
long-term/post-acute care
(LTPAC), 12–14
assisted living facilities (ALF),
12–13
continuous care retirement
communities (CCRC), 13
home health agencies
(HHA), 13
hospice centers, 13
independent rehabilitation
facilities (IRF), 13
long-term acute-care hospitals
(LTACH), 14
skilled/nursing facilities (SNF),
13–14
outpatient/ambulatory care, 12
Healthcare providers, 9–10

Healthcare regulations, 17
Health Information Technology
for Economic and Clinical
Health (HITECH) Act, 17, 19
Health Insurance Portability and
Accountability Act of 1996
(HIPAA), 17
Health Level Seven (HL7), 43
Health maintenance organizations
(HMOs), 8–9
Health savings accounts, 9
Help-desk, 139, 140
HFMA, *see* Healthcare
Financial Management
Association (HFMA)
HHA, *see* Home Health
Agencies (HHA)
HHS, *see* Health and Human
Services (HHS)
HIMSS Analytics, 47
HIPAA, *see* Health Insurance
Portability and
Accountability Act of 1996
(HIPAA)
HIS, *see* Disrupted healthcare
information systems
(HIS) operations; Normal
healthcare information
systems (HIS) operations
HITECH, *see* Health Information
Technology for Economic
and Clinical Health
(HITECH) Act
HL7, *see* Health Level Seven (HL7)
HMOs, *see* Health maintenance
organizations (HMOs)
Home- and community-based
services (HCBS), xv
Home Health Agencies (HHA),
xiv–xv, xvii, xx, xxi, 45–46
Home Health Resource Groups, xvii
Hospice, xv
Hospital Reductions Program, 161

Hospitals, 11–12
  location, 11–12
  ownership type
    private, 11
    public/government-managed, 11
  service type, 11
  teaching status, 11

ICD, *see* International Statistical
    Classification of
    Diseases (ICD)
ILFs, *see* Independent living
    facilities (ILFs)
IMPACT, *see* Improving Medicare Post-
    Acute Care Transformation
    (IMPACT) Act
Implementation, 95
Implementation manager, 133–134
Implementation support
    specialist, 134
Improving Medicare Post-Acute
    Care Transformation
    (IMPACT) Act, 19, 43
Independent living facilities
    (ILFs), 45
Information system maturity, 46–48
Information technology (IT),
    125–131
  budget, 126
  documentation, 126–128
    department, 127–128
    operational, 127
    system, 127
  projects, 129–131
  roles, 132–134
    EHR, 133–134
    general, 132–133
    healthcare, 133
    senior management, 132
  strategic plan, 125–126
    efforts, 126
    gap analysis, 125–126
    map, 125

system performance, 128–129
  baseline assessment, 128
  software evaluation, 128–129
  technical and information needs
    recommendations, 129
Inpatient rehabilitation facility (IRF),
    xiv, xvii
Institute of Medicine, 151
Insurance, 35
Integration testing, 91
Interface engine, 94–95
International Commonwealth Fund,
    170–171, 172
International landscapes, on LTPAC
    HIT, 169–185
  International Commonwealth
    Fund, 170–171
  overview, 169–170
  surveying, 171–185
    Asia, 183–184
    Australia, 182–183
    Europe, 184–185
    North America, 172, 175, 182
International Standards
    Organization (ISO), 28–29
International Statistical
    Classification of Diseases
    (ICD), 43
Internet service provider (ISP), 31
IRF, *see* inpatient rehabilitation
    facility (IRF)
ISO, *see* International Standards
    Organization (ISO)
ISP, *see* Internet service provider (ISP)
Issue tracking, 139
IT, *see* Information technology (IT)
    and LTPAC
IT-based certifications, 135

Just-in-time training, 94

Kaiser Permanente (KP), 6
Kets de Vries, Manfred F. R., 120

Kotter, John P., 116
KP, *see* Kaiser Permanente (KP)

LANs, *see* Local area networks (LANs)
Laws and regulations, 17–20
Leadership, 117–124
    archetypes, 120–121
    culture, 119–120
    guardrails, 121–124
        business ethics, 124
        business operations, 122–123
        legal and regulatory
            compliance, 123–124
        setting strategy, 117–118
Leadership rounding, 119
Lean, 68
Legal and regulatory compliance,
        123–124
Length of stay (LOS), 148
Like for like approach, 87
Local area networks (LANs), 31
Longitudinal Electronic Health
        Record, 162
Longitudinal health records, 160–161
Long-term acute-care hospital
        (LTACH), xiv, xvii, xx, 14
Long-term/post-acute care (LTPAC),
        xiii, xxvii, 12
    assisted living facilities (ALF),
        12–13
    continuous care retirement
        communities (CCRC), 13
    and future, 145–165
        overview, 145–147
        person-centered models,
            151–158
        person-centered outcome
            measures, 158–161
        valued quality coordination of
            care (VQCC), 148–151
        value propositions, 161–163
    and healthcare environment,
        3–23

delivery of healthcare
    services, 16–22
    overview, 3–4
    patients/consumers, 5–7
    U.S. payers and providers, 7–16
home health agencies (HHA), 13
hospice centers, 13
independent rehabilitation
    facilities (IRF), 13
international landscapes on,
    169–185
    International Commonwealth
        Fund, 170–171
    overview, 169–170
    surveying, 171–185
long-term acute-care hospitals
    (LTACH), 14
privacy and security, 101–110
    CIA triad, 102–103
    data governance, 104–105
    data management controls,
        105–107
    disaster recovery and business
        continuity plan, 108–109
    overview, 101–102
    risk, 107–108
    user access controls, 106–107
and SDLC, 55–80, 83–99
    acquisition, 73–78
    decision, 57–63
    overview, 56–57
    project management, 83–99
    selection, 63–73
skilled/nursing facilities (SNF),
    13–14
and technology environment,
    27–51
    application needs, 44–46
    applications, 34–44
    information system maturity,
        46–48
    infrastructure, 30–33
    overview, 27–30

LOS, *see* Length of stay (LOS)
LTACH, *see* Long-term acute-care
   hospital (LTACH)
LTPAC, *see* Long-term/post-acute
   care (LTPAC)

MACRA, *see* Medicare Access and
   CHIP Reauthorization Act
   (MACRA)
Management, 124–140
   external relationships, 138–140
   operations, 124–131
      budget, 126
      documentation, 126–128
      projects, 129–131
      strategic plan, 125–126
      system performance, 128–129
   staff, 131–138
Manual testing, 89
Marketing, 45, 46
Market segmentation, 5–6
MDS, *see* Minimum Data Set (MDS)
Meaningful Use program, *see*
   Medicare and Medicaid
   EHR Incentive Program
Medicaid, 21
Medicare, 21
Medicare Access and CHIP
   Reauthorization Act
   (MACRA), 19–20
Medicare and Medicaid EHR
   Incentive Program, 105
Medication management, 44, 150
Merit-Based Inentive Payment
   System (MIPS), 20
Merriam–Webster's Dictionary, 160
Metadata management, 69
Minimum Data Set (MDS), 44, 149
MIPS, *see* Merit-Based Inentive
   Payment System (MIPS)
Mission statement, 118
Missouri Quality Improvement
   Initiative (MOQI), 162

National Evaluation System for health
   Technology (NEST), 22
Nolan, R. L., 46
Non-financial benchmarks, 123
Normal healthcare information
   systems (HIS) operations,
   96–97
North America, 172, 175, 182
Nursing Home Reform Act, 18
Nursing homes, 44–45

OBRA '87, *see* Omnibus Budget
   Reconciliation Act of 1987
   (OBRA '87)
Occupational Safety and Health
   Administration (OSHA), 22
Office for Civil Rights (OCR), 21
Office of the National Coordinator
   (ONC), 19, 21, 133, 148
Omnibus Budget Reconciliation Act
   of 1987 (OBRA '87), 18
ONC, *see* Office of the National
   Coordinator (ONC)
Open Systems Interconnection
   (OSI), 28, 30, 34, 48, 49
Operational documentation, 127
Operational testing, 91
OSHA, *see* Occupational Safety
   and Health Administration
   (OSHA)
OSI, *see* Open Systems
   Interconnection (OSI)
OSI-model layer-3 function, 31

Participating provider options
   (PPOs), 9
Patient scheduling, 45, 46
Patients/consumers, 5–7
Payers, 8–9
Payroll system, 35–36
PCP, *see* Primary care physician (PCP)
Performance evaluation, 137–138
Personal funds, 9

Personal health records (PHR), 40–41
Person-centered medical homes, 15
Person-centered models, 151–158
Person-centered outcome measures, 158–161
  experience, 159–160
  longitudinal health records, 160–161
  partnership, 159
Person-Centric eLongitudinal Spectrum of Care, 60
Person encounter data, 6
Phased approach, 87
PHR, *see* Personal health records (PHR)
Physical safeguards, 106
Pilot approach, 87
Point-of-service (POS), 9
Policies and procedures (P&P) documents, 127–128
Polypharmacy, 150
Portable devices, 32–33
POS, *see* Point-of-service (POS)
Post-implementation, 96–98
  disrupted HIS operations, 97–98
  normal HIS operations, 96–97
P&P, *see* Policies and procedures (P&P) documents
PPOs, *see* Participating provider options (PPOs)
Practice workflow/information management redesign specialist, 133
Pre-implementation, 84–95
  activation, 94–95
  change management, 86
  planning, 85
  solution customization, 87–93
  strategies, 86–87
  system integration, 93–94
  training, 94
  user and operational manuals, 94

Primary care physician (PCP), 9
Privacy and security, 101–110
  CIA triad, 102–103
  data governance, 104–105
  data management controls, 105–107
  disaster recovery and business continuity plan, 108–109
  overview, 101–102
  risk, 107–108
  user access controls, 106–107
Private hospitals, 11
Private insurance, 8–9
Project manager, 130
Psychiatric hospitals, 11
Public/government-managed hospitals, 11
Purchase, *see* Person encounter data

RAI, *see* Resident Assessment Instrument (RAI)
RAP, *see* Request for anticipated payment (RAP)
Raw data, 30
RCS-I, *see* Resident Classification System, Version I (RCS-I)
Real estate investment trust (REIT), 59
Real-time data integration, 93
Recovery point objective (RPO), 66
Recovery time objective (RTO), 66
Reference and master data management, 69
Regression testing, 91
Regulatory bodies, 20–22
Rehabilitation hospitals, 11
REIT, *see* Real estate investment trust (REIT)
Request for anticipated payment (RAP), 46
Request for information (RFI), 75–76
Request for proposal (RFP), 75–76
Request tracking, 139

Resident Assessment Instrument
    (RAI), 18
Resident Classification System,
    Version I (RCS-I), 20
Resource Utilization Groups (RUGs),
    20, xvii
Response times, 67
Revenue and expenses, 122
RFI, *see* Request for information (RFI)
RFP, *see* Request for proposal (RFP)
Risk, 107–108
Road map analysis, 77
Routers and switches, 30–31
RPO, *see* Recovery point
    objective (RPO)
RTO, *see* Recovery time
    objective (RTO)
RUGs, *see* Resource Utilization
    Groups (RUGs)

Safety measures, 159
Scheduled data integration, 93
Scope creep, 131
SDLC, *see* Systems development life
    cycle (SDLC)
Security and data encryption, 66
Security audits, 91
Senior IT security leader, 104
Senior Segmentation Algorithm, 6
Servers, 30–31
Service desk, 96
Service-Level Agreement (SLA), 139
SIS, *see* Strategic information
    systems (SIS)
Six Sigma, 61, 68
Skilled nursing facility (SNF), xiv,
    xvii, xx, xxi, 20, 45, 151, 163
SLA, *see* Service-Level
    Agreement (SLA)
SNF, *see* Skilled nursing facility (SNF)
SNOMED CT, *see* Systematic
    Nomenclature of Medicine
    (SNOMED) Clinical Terms

Software evaluation, 128–129
Software support technician, 134
Static clinical data, 160
Statistical computation
    programs, 5
Strategic information systems
    (SIS), 62
Strategic plan, 125–126
    efforts, 126
    gap analysis, 125–126
    map, 125
Stress testing, 91
Surgical hospitals, 11
Survey & Certification Group, 109
System and network
    architecture, 66
Systematic Nomenclature of
    Medicine (SNOMED)
    Clinical Terms, 43
System backups, 67
System configuration
    management, 96
System documentation, 127
System integration, 68
System monitoring, 67
System performance, 128–129
    baseline assessment, 128
    software evaluation, 128–129
    technical and information needs
        recommendations, 129
Systems development life cycle
    (SDLC) and LTPAC
    acquisition, 73–78
    build, 75
    buy, 75
    decision, 57–63
        defining problem, 59–61
        determining cause, 61
        identifying solutions, 61–63
    overview, 56–57
    project management, 83–99
        implementation, 95
        overview, 84

post-implementation, 96–98
pre-implementation, 84–95
selection, 63–73
analysis of alternatives, 72
preliminary investigation,
63–65
proposal/approval, 72–73
requirements analysis, 65–71
System testing, 91

Teaching hospitals, 11
Technical safeguards, 106
Technology environment, and
LTPAC, 27–51
application needs, 44–46
applications, 34–44
administrative, 34–35
clinical, 36–41
financial, 35–36
standardized data elements,
43–44
standards and interoperability,
41–43
information system maturity,
46–48
infrastructure, 30–33
client terminals, 32–33
data, 30
data storage and data
integration, 33
portable devices, 32–33
routers and switches, 30–31
servers, 30–31
wired and wireless networks,
31–32
overview, 27–30
Technology infrastructure, 30–33
client terminals, 32–33
data, 30
data storage and data
integration, 33
portable devices, 32–33
routers and switches, 30–31

servers, 30–31
wired and wireless networks,
31–32
Telehealth and telemedicine, 184
Testing activities, 88–93
controls, 91–92
levels, 90–91
methodology, 88–90
reports, 92–93
Through the Patients Eyes, 152
Time zone and daylight savings
time support, 67
ToC, *see* Transitions of care (ToC)
Trainer, 134
Training, 94
Training and in-service
programs, 135
Transitions of care (ToC), 42
Triple-A approach, 107
"Triple Aim of Healthcare", 146–147

Unit testing, 90
University hospitals, 11
User access controls, 106–107
User and operational manuals, 94
User satisfaction surveys, 139

Valued quality coordination of care
(VQCC), 148–151
chronic care comorbidity care,
149–150
duration of care, 148–149
eAssessments, 149
medication management, 150
technology, 150–151
Value propositions, 161–163
Value statement, 118, 119
Vendor management, 138–139
Vendor solutions, 64
Version control, 91
Vision statement, 118
Visiting nurse association, *see* Home
Health Agencies (HHA)

VQCC, *see* Valued quality
    coordination of care (VQCC)

WANs, *see* Wide area networks
    (WANs)
Web-based platforms, 175

Web browsing technology, 183
White-box testing, 90
Wide area networks (WANs), 31
Wired and wireless networks, 31–32
Workflow, 68, 96
Written and oral communications, 119

Printed in the United States
by Baker & Taylor Publisher Services